❦ FINDING THE VOICE INSIDE

Writing as a Spiritual Quest for Women

GAIL COLLINS-RANADIVE

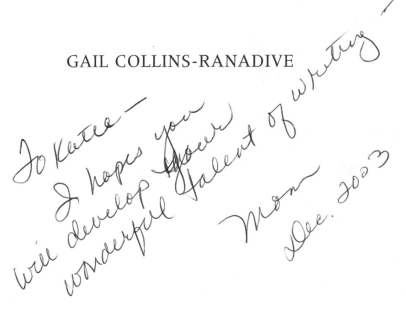

To Katee —
I hopes you
will develop your
wonderful talent of writing
Mom
Dec. 2003

SKINNER HOUSE BOOKS
BOSTON

The first edition of this book was titled *Writing Re-creatively: A Spiritual Quest for Women*.

Printed in Canada

Cover design by Kathryn Sky-Peck
Text design by Sandra Rigney
Author photo by Bill Ward

ISBN 1-55896-430-4

Library of Congress Cataloging-in-Publication Data

Ranadive, Gail, 1944-
    Finding the voice inside : writing as a spiritual quest for women / Gail Collins-Ranadive.
        p. cm.
    Includes bibliographical references.
    ISBN 1-55896-430-4 (alk. paper)
    1. Women—Religious life. 2. Spiritual journals—Authorship. I. Title.

BL625.7 .C49 2002
200'.82—dc21   2002022679

10 9 8 7 6 5 4 3 2 1
05 04 03 02

 The author wishes to express her gratitude to the Unitarian Universalist Women's Federation for a 1991 Feminist Theology Award that helped make this book possible. Special thanks to Stacy Tuthill, Carolyn Cottom, Betty Jo Middleton, Mary Benard, and Kathy Braeman for their editorial advice and assistance.

Some of these poems have appeared in the following publications: *American Literary, Earth's Daughters, Folio, Friendly Woman*, and *The Unitarian Universalist Poets*, Pudding House, 1996.

For, of, and by
the feminine
arising among us

TABLE OF CONTENTS

INTRODUCTION

WRITERS FREQUENTLY SAY that the hardest part of writing is the blank page at the beginning. Even harder is when the page isn't blank at all, when it has been filled with someone else's words and someone else's experiences. This is the female writer's challenge. Our world has been named, defined, and constructed from the male perspective, as if that were universal. Our experience of the world is different from men's, beginning at birth.

This book is about clearing that page and starting again in our own words, *finding the voice inside*. Women are looking for ways to stop fitting ourselves sideways into history, sociology, spirituality, and philosophy as conceived by and for men. We need to balance that male worldview and to reclaim our own feminine spirituality. To do that, we must first re-create the images, symbols, and metaphors of our own lives as women. Writing is a way into this important work, for writing sets our inner knowing outside of ourselves, where we can reflect upon it as something real. Writing becomes our spiritual discipline.

The writing exercises that follow are open-ended. See what catches your attention, then hold it, contemplate it, and contemplate yourself within it. In other words, take a long, honest look at what's real, and then begin to write about it without censoring what wants to come out onto the blank paper. Just get out of the way, so that your embodied life experience can become the basic material for spiritual reflection, the flesh becoming word. Writing can be the reflexive moment that begins the journey toward healing and wholeness, but it is only phase one of the spiritual quest. The goal is to move you from the poetic revelation to something beyond your own conscious will, to call you to a new dimension of life, the word become flesh.

Writing as a spiritual quest can be done alone or in a group setting. For each exercise, you will write for eight to ten minutes on a given topic. Regardless of whether you are doing these exercises alone or with a group, I encourage you to read your writing aloud. Writing alone in a journal is a long-tested spiritual discipline technique through which one can talk to God/dess, Gracious Spirit, Spirit of Grace (whatever form divinity takes for you) *and listen* to the reply, via the "aha!s" and insights that come through while doing this writing on a regular basis, say every morning as a centering exercise. If you are using this book with a group, you will want some ground rules. I suggest that no one be allowed to comment on what others have written and that everyone be free to pass but encouraged not to. It may help you to look at the writing samples at the end of the book to see how others have interpreted and responded to these exercises.

There are forty exercises in all. You may decide to do one exercise per session and use the extra time for discussion. Do whatever works best for you. You will evolve your own sense of bonding and your own dynamic. You may even develop additional writing exercises on a new topic that has opened up for you.

Each exercise is titled with an *re-* word, to indicate the process of restoration to a previous condition. As we write, we are not creating something out of nothing. Rather, we are tapping into something that's already within us, waiting to be reawakened and given voice. It is time to begin.

ONE

RETREAT TO A SAFE PLACE

Retreat: *to withdraw from something hazardous or unpleasant, fall back*

AS YOU COME TOGETHER FOR THE FIRST TIME, or as you begin this work alone, find a way to make the space sacred. Perhaps you'll choose to light a candle as a symbol of the living presence that is both within and beyond our own being. It can also be a way to focus, to center yourself in the moment. Our word for focus comes from the Latin word for fireplace, the hearth at the center of the home. And the sacred fire was brought to the home from the temple of Vesta, the Greeks' Hestia, Goddess of the Hearth who personifies the archetype of the Self.

Knowing that everything written and read in this space will remain here, how will you identify yourself?

Begin by writing an introduction of yourself. You might choose to follow a standard I.D. format, giving your name, occupation, size, age, colorings, etc., perhaps adding some things you'd like to see included, such as vocation, parental status, etc.

In Western cultures, we often choose to identify ourselves through what we do and give our qualifications to authorize our work. In many Eastern cultures, one is often identified through one's relationship within a family. For instance, it has been the cus-

1

tom in India for the son's new wife to change her last name to his, her middle name to his first name, and her first name to whatever new name her in-laws choose for her. My in-laws call me "Nilakshi," girl with the blue eyes. But my brother-in-law always and only calls me "Vahini," sister-in-law.

Identify, describe, introduce yourself, on paper. What do you want others to know about you? Or, what do you want to say about yourself to yourself?

Read aloud what you have written. Remember, do not interrupt yourself or anyone else with comments, explanations, or reactions. Simply listen to what has come up and out through the hand onto the page. ❧

TWO

RECONSIDER WHO YOU REALLY ARE

Reconsider: *to consider (to deliberate upon, examine; to think or dream; to believe or judge) again*

FILLING OUT THE CONVENTIONAL I.D. FORM requires using the analytic side of the brain: the side that separates the whole picture into its constituent parts.

But we have another side to our brain: the side that perceives analogically. This is the side that comprehends complex wholes instantly and intuitively. By imagining similarities between dissimilar things, this part of the brain sees more than what literally meets the eye.

My analytical identity names my academic qualifications, describes my teaching experience, and lists my published work. But analogically, I now identify with the columbine, an image from the natural world that is a metaphor for the larger self I am called to become.

Columba is Latin for *dove*, and reflects the flower's resemblance to the bird of peace.

A woman's rebirth journey was once symbolized by the image of a dove coming out of a dolphin's mouth (*delphos*: womb). That *Jonah* is a cognate of *dove* in Hebrew gives me a biblical image to use around my own issue of resistance. The dove also symbolizes

3

the Holy Spirit. Its manifestation in the delicate wildflower has become an important symbol for my spiritual life.

Explore an image from nature, animal, vegetable, or mineral, that best describes who you are at this time in your life, here and now. Read aloud what you have written. ❧

THREE

REGARD YOUR IMAGE

Regard: *to look at attentively; to gaze upon*

YOUR IMAGE OF THE SACRED can become your spiritual companion, guiding you into deeper truths about your life than those in the realm of ego consciousness and willpower. For the spiritual journey takes place in the interior world, a world that can be entered through the "other" senses, such as imagination, insight, intuition, inspiration, inclination. Your image can become your vehicle for entering this other world, especially if it is large enough to move from image to symbol to metaphor to myth and/or religious narrative.

This is an invitation to go deeper, to open to/be opened by a process of revelation that is ongoing both in the personal spiritual narrative and in the collective religious story of the wider culture. Research your image in places such as *The Herder Dictionary of Symbols* and Barbara G. Walker's *The Women's Encyclopedia of Myths and Secrets*. Even a dictionary that contains the roots of words is a good place to look. For example, *The American Heritage Dictionary* gives the root of *columbine* as coming from the Latin word for *dove*.

For me, the delicate image of the columbine with its symbolic dove grew into an organizing metaphor that was to contain my spiritual journey throughout the years I spent attending seminary.

Seminary, that place for the training of priests, rabbis, and ministers, comes from the Latin root *seminarium*, which refers to seed-plot, garden, nursery. Thus seminary for me became the place for cultivating the inner life, for growing the spiritual Self. Your image from nature can become a symbol of transcendence, pointing to a need for liberation from a state of being that is too immature, too fixed, too final.

You will have to learn to trust what your sacred image is telling you that you may not want to know that you know. So choose/be chosen by it carefully.

Write about what your chosen image reveals to you about the sacred. What does it say about your relationship to the sacred? Read aloud what you have written. ❧

FOUR

REDEEM YOUR SHADOW

Redeem: *to recover ownership; to set free, rescue*

AS YOU BEGIN TO GO EVER DEEPER, you come to the first layers of who you have become: The person you've fashioned to present to the world has been informed by the "oughts" and "shoulds" of society, as well as by a need for love and acceptance. It is also in the image of the self you may most want to be. But for whatever reasons we try to live in ways we admire rather than from who we really are, there comes a point when these acquired "gifts" turn on us, and become *gifft*, the German word for poison, as surely as a continual chemical altering of a personality becomes an addiction.

We can only fake it for so long through sheer willpower. That something is radically wrong manifests itself in addictions, eating disorders, chronic illnesses, suicidal thinking, and depression: all signs that the primary Self (the Soul) has been silenced, stuffed, denied, disclaimed, devalued, violated.

Anger, resentment, fear, blaming, despair, and hopelessness are the fruits of keeping the real self locked away.

The persona we project into the world casts its corresponding shadow in the personal, unconscious part of our psyches, Jung tells us. This shadow contains the cut-off parts of ourselves that we didn't dare or care to claim. At first glance, the shadow would appear to hold mainly what's negative: in fact, it is holding what is positive hostage. It takes an enormous amount of courage to go down through the shadow material in order to retrieve the essential gift it contains.

Explore in writing an image of the sacred for suggestions of its negative aspect. For example, water is both life-sustaining and yet capable of drowning a living thing. A rock is both reliably solid and yet rigid. Do not be afraid to look at how this may reflect your own shadow stuff. Read aloud what you have written.

FIVE

RE-ENTER THAT OTHER COUNTRY

Re-enter: *to enter a second or subsequent time*

AS WE ARE ALL AWARE, our present world has come to prefer, value, and rely upon the side of the brain that deals with analytic thinking. This was not necessarily always the case. In *The Underside of History*, Elise Boulding claims there is strong evidence to suggest that our forebears used both sides of the brain equally. They were ambidextrous until the Paleolithic period, when they shifted to right-handedness as hunters. At that time, the left hand, and the side of the brain that controlled it, became less used and increasingly devalued. A dualism based on the use of the right and left hand began to evolve:

right	left
strong	weak
day	night
male	female
life	death
good	evil
high	low
sacred	profane

When this dualism became irreversible, Boulding points out, the image of women (as non-hunters? as still ambidextrous?) became permanently fixed on the "negative" side of the listing. Male superiority and dominance began in earnest.

In order to retrieve what got lost while language was developing out of the analytic side of the brain, we must re-enter what feminist literary critic Helene Cixous calls "that other limitless country." It is that unconscious place where the repressed (women? fairies?) has "managed to survive."

Write about that which cannot, or has not, been named. Is there something you sense vaguely, below the level of articulation, something you act out of? Read aloud what you have written. ❧

SIX

RECOVER YOUR FAVORITE TREE

Recover: *to get back; to regain*

AS WOMEN IN A MALE-DOMINATED CULTURE, we know in our bones that the language we speak is of, for, and by our fathers, brothers, husbands, lovers, sons. We know this when we become frustrated, angry, or invisible when the men we love can't hear/don't grasp what we are trying to say. And so, more often than not, we give up and continue to fit ourselves into the images, symbols, metaphors, and myths of our male-oriented culture, which define us only in relationship to the male "norm."

In doing so, we do violence to who we ourselves are. Living in the formlessness that exists below the level of language, we have no words that name who we are to shape into stories, and therefore we cannot make meaning out of our life experiences. We remain in the limitless country, silent and silenced.

In her book *Stealing the Language*, Alicia Ostriker tells us that women poets are continually trying to make the language say what they need it to say. Is this possible? By going back to the roots of words, we often find they began as visual images. For example, a daisy is a day's eye; disaster means to be separated from the stars. Before becoming fixed, each word was a figurative image that activated the analogic part of the brain.

11

Write about a tree. What kind of tree comes to mind? Is it a specific tree, perhaps one out of your childhood? What is your relationship to it? What does it symbolize for you? Does it want to become a metaphor? For what? Let the tree take you where it wants to go. (I chose the word tree here because, while I was studying with one of his original pupils in Europe, I learned that Carl Jung found that many of his female analysands pictured their psychological/spiritual selves as trees.) Read aloud what you have written. ❧

SEVEN

REINFORCE YOUR CONSCIOUS EFFORTS

Reinforce: *to strengthen; to support*

DREAMS HAVE BEEN CALLED the workshop of evolution by Hungarian psychiatrist Sandor Ferenczi, who suggested that "human beings may have evolved in large measure because our ancestors first initiated and explored the psycho-biological innovation of articulate speech in their dreams." Jeremy Taylor, with whom I studied dream work in seminary, claims that an astonishingly large number of the cultural ideas and scientific innovations that have shaped our contemporary world were born first as inspirations in dreams. Ah, but you don't dream, you say? . . . not that you remember anyway. Yet you *do* dream, whether you remember them or not.

Why do we dream? Well, it would seem that our psyches need to work things out on levels other than what our ego-conscious minds can allow, or deal with, or grasp. It's as though our God-Selves, our Souls, are showing us their particular paths, telling us about our larger lives. It's as though the life force of the universe, of which we are but the eyes and ears and voice, is working out its next manifestation through us. It's as though God/dess, Divinity, the Sacred is speaking directly through the stuff of our own lives. And this all happens through the medium of dreams. Joseph

Campbell claims that *a dream is a private myth; a myth is a public dream.*

All dreams come in the service of health and wholeness, Jeremy Taylor assures us, even the nightmares—especially the nightmares! These are an effort to get our attention.

Dream work is done most effectively within a small group of others who are also doing this inner work. As we listen to one another, and reflect back what we hear—"if this were my dream...."—we can hold the dreamer accountable to things in the dream the ego-self doesn't want to pay attention to, thus accessing another layer of knowing and growing.

Describe in writing a recent dream, or even a snatch of one. Read aloud what you have written. Keep a dream journal and pen beside your bed; this signals to your subconscious mind that you are ready to listen to what it has to tell you, especially as it reinforces what you know during waking hours. ❧

EIGHT

RESURRECT THE SERPENT

Resurrect: *to bring back to life; to bring back into practice, notice, or use*

IMAGES THAT LIE DEEP WITHIN OUR PSYCHES cannot be dealt with on a rational level, out of the analytical part of the brain. As Nelle Morton notes in *The Journey Is Home*, an image is not merely a mental picture; it is a dynamic through which both an individual and the body politic communicate. Images shape lifestyles and values, one's sense of self and of structures of power. They take on a life of their own, beyond our conscious control.

Take, for instance, the image of the serpent. No matter how hard I try, I cannot seem to overcome my aversion to snakes, no doubt left over from my Protestant upbringing. Yet I recall the sterling silver caduceus on the charm bracelet I wore as an off-duty student nurse; its serpent was a symbol of health and healing. Today, I also know that the serpent was once associated with the goddess and the feminine power of life. The shedding of the serpent's skin and the monthly shedding of the lining of a woman's womb both symbolize renewal. I know this intellectually. But when I come across newly emerged water snakes in the wildlife sanctuary I frequent, I have to use every ounce of willpower to stand my ground and not run in the other direction!

Can we retrieve the images that the patriarchy has coopted and often actually turned against us women? Barbara G. Walker's *The Woman's Dictionary of Symbols and Sacred Objects* begins this process. In one of her twenty-seven entries on the serpent, she reveals that the serpent/hair of Medusa symbolized menstrual mysteries, the knowledge of which could turn men to stone. The blood of the beheaded Medusa gave birth to Pegasus, the winged horse of poetic inspiration. It is only through a poetic revision (seeing again) of the images that we can begin to disrupt the subliminal hold they have over us.

Write about the serpent; let the image lead your words to where they want to go. Read aloud what you have written. ❧

NINE

REALIGN YOURSELF WITH THE SERPENT

Realign: *to reproduce a proper relationship or condition*

THE SERPENT HAS LONG BEEN ASSOCIATED with the feminine aspect of divinity. Ancient images of the goddess often depict serpents entwined in her robes, decorating her ornaments, or held in her hands. Today, the serpent's reappearance in women's dreams seems to symbolize the resurgent power of the feminine. This is the power to regenerate and renew, as the serpent does with the shedding of its skin, and woman the lining of her womb.

As women assert their power over their own lives and claim their own authority, snake dreams grow more common. It's as if an ally has appeared. Claiming one's own serpent power means having the courage to shed that which is constricting one's inner growth. This often produces profound conflict and anguish.

Men self-differentiate through separation and autonomy; thus their spiritual wholeness means moving towards a unitive experience. Because women self-differentiate through relating with and identifying through others, our spiritual unfolding demands just the opposite: we must become the "parted one."

The Latin verb *videre* means *to part* and is the word from which *widow* is derived, a word etymologically related to the words *individual, indivisible, individuation*. But to separate from those we love in order to use our energy for our own inner work frankly feels just awful. It contradicts everything we have come to accept as moral and good. It's as if we find ourselves being tempted again by the serpent in the Garden of Eden. This time, perhaps we can accept the snake as our ally, instead of as our enemy.

A common dream sequence reported by women is that of Christ coming down from the cross, walking away, and a serpent climbing up onto it to take his place. Describe yourself in writing as a serpent. Read aloud what you have written. ❧

TEN

REVIEW A BIBLICAL IMAGE

Review: *to look over or study again; to examine with an eye to criticism or correction; to reconsider*

JOSEPH CAMPBELL PROPOSES in *Myths to Live By* that all the great religions and mythologies of the world are actually poems that are to be interpreted figuratively rather than literally. Reading his book was a turning point in my life. I had been struggling to understand how and why I kept finding stories that paralleled my Christian heritage in the books I brought back from India for my children. In them were virgin births, savior figures walking on water, great floods, etc. Clearly there was something deep within the human psyche that transcended particular cultures. But why?

Campbell outlines four reasons for myths and religions in the human experience. First, there's the cosmological function: to define a people's place in the universe. The second function of myth is sociological: to define the individual's place within the culture into which one has been born. Next comes the psychological function: to guide a person through all the stages of a useful life. And finally, there is a spiritual dimension to myths: to give one an actual experience of the transcendent mystery, whatever one chooses to call it.

Untoward things happen when people accept their religious stories as literally true and everyone else's as false, pagan, heretical, heathen, or misguided. But what happens if we reread our culture's stories as poems, from the analogic part of the brain?

The good news about figurative language is this: It is dynamic, open-ended, growing, changeable. There are as many interpretations of a poem as there are readers. Does it really matter what the poet meant? Often the ambiguous words and images in the poem were used so that the reader might grasp what's going on in her or his own life at that moment.

Recall a biblical image, metaphor, parable, or story and use it in your writing in a way that is new for you. Read aloud what you have written. ❧

ELEVEN

REVIVE YOUR EARLIER SELF

Revive: *to bring or come back to life or consciousness; to impart or regain vigor or spirit*

JOSEPH CAMPBELL REMINDS US that we human beings are born some twelve years too soon. Unlike our animal counterparts, we cannot survive on our own for many years after our birth. Therefore, we are born into families, as a sort of second womb.

Those early years can be filled with wonder as we acquire the fundamentals of human culture. Every day becomes an adventure as we learn and experience and grow physically, psychologically, and intellectually. These are truly magical years!

Yet two recent studies commissioned by the American Association of University Women report on a disturbing phenomenon revealed in their research: somewhere around the age of eleven, girls seem to come up against a wall that blocks their further learning and unfolding. Why? The research shows that between elementary and middle school, girls become aware of the dichotomy between what their parents and teachers encourage them to do and be and what society will actually allow them to do and be in their lives. At this point, girls begin to withdraw and internalize that they are not as good, as smart, as capable as their brothers. This process reinforces itself. As a girl stops speaking up in class or claims that she doesn't know the answer (which she did know a year earlier), she is called on less and less and becomes more and more invisible. Her self-esteem plummets; depression sets in; eating disorders develop. Whereas adolescence is a time when boys open up to the possibilities life offers, for girls it can become a time of closing down in order to fit into the limited role society demands of females: sugar and spice and everything nice, silence, and compliance.

Try to recapture, with words, the person you were becoming before you were socialized to be otherwise. Read aloud what you have written. ❧

TWELVE

REFLECT ON A CHILDHOOD RITUAL

Reflect: *to mirror or become mirrored; to manifest as a result of one's ac-*
tions; to think or consider seriously; to bring blame or reproach

NOT UNLIKE OUR ANIMAL COUNTERPARTS, we humans are im-
printed by the rites, rituals, and taboos of society through our families. Just as rituals brought order into our personal childhoods,
there is comfort in knowing that certain things will happen at the
same time in the same place each day, such as the bedtime story.
Somehow, when there's order outside of ourselves, we can bring
order to the chaos within ourselves as well. Family rituals, even
those we detest, bring stability to our lives. We know without a
doubt what is expected of us and when, if not always why. The explanations don't always make sense, of course: changing under-
wear daily in case you get into a accident, cleaning up your plate
because people are starving in—, etc. But they remain ingrained in
our psyches, and we continue to reenact them in our daily lives,
often unconsciously. Often any change will bring discomfort, resistance, disorientation.

For example, I was raised to eat with a knife, fork, and spoon.
But when I'm visiting my in-laws in India, I'm expected to eat with
my fingers, using only my right hand. (The left hand is taboo. I am,
naturally, left-handed.) In fact, so much in Indian culture is oppo-

site from what I was taught in my New England home that I wrote a children's book in an effort to sort it all out! And I'll never forget visiting a mosque in New Delhi and taking off my shoes. The two Philadelphia schoolteachers in the tour group looked down at my stockinged feet and exclaimed, "You must be from Boston!" It has taken me a long time to learn to be comfortable wearing sandals, without stockings, in public: I feel naked.

Re-examine a rite, ritual, or taboo you've carried since childhood and write about it. Do you know the rationale behind it? Does it matter? What did you pass on to your children? Why? Why not? What did you/would you change? Read aloud what you have written. ❧

THIRTEEN
RECOUNT A FAMILY STORY

Recount: *to narrate the facts or particulars of*

FAMILY STORIES ARE ANOTHER METHOD by which we become socialized, humanized, civilized. The tales told to us about our kin
and our place in the clan transmit family values and present us
with role models either to emulate or to reject. Through the stories
we're told about courtship, lost fortunes, and survival, we are expected to take our place in the next generation. Do we go on to further the family ideals? Or do we become the black sheep? No
matter how we finally live out our own lives, we remain connected
to our family of origin, for better or for worse. We cannot divorce
our family heritage.

The family name "Ranadive" means "glory of the battlefield,"
and it reflects that my former husband was born into the warrior
caste of Hinduism. So it should have come as no great surprise that
he got drafted into the U.S. Army (before becoming a U.S. citizen!)
and enjoyed a twenty-three-year career in the military. But it was
a surprise to me. Without knowing why, I found I was very uncomfortable being part of the military. In an attempt to come to
terms with this, I took classes in military history and national security policy and eventually ended up earning a master's degree in
Peace Studies. I worked with the campaign that lobbied the

National Peace Academy bill through Congress in 1985. Yet it was seven years later that I learned the following about my mother's ancestry: Heinrich and Rachel Stief, a couple of Dutch-Baltic origin, left Europe in the early 1770s to avoid religious persecution. They were members of a devout Protestant sect that believed in simplicity of worship, communal living, and pacifism. Upon arriving in Philadelphia, they learned that, with the American Revolution impending, men were about to be required to do compulsory military service. So they emigrated to Canada, with their seven sons. I finally feel "at home" within my family heritage.

Begin to reclaim a family story that helped shape you, consciously or unconsciously, by writing it down. Read aloud what you have written. ❧

FOURTEEN

REFINE A SEASONAL CUSTOM

Refine: *to purify*

ONE STEP BEYOND THE FAMILY STORIES that shape us are the folk tales (fables, legends, nursery rhymes, epics, fairy tales) we hear as children. In *Children and Books*, May Hill Arbuthnot discusses this accumulated wisdom of ordinary "folk" as an effort to understand natural events, deal with other people, and express universally experienced emotions. Folk tales contain elements of older religions, historical events, rituals, and superstitions. They serve as "the cement of society" by mirroring morality: good will triumph over evil.

One of the theories of the origin of folk tales holds that they are the remnants of the pagan (country folk) beliefs forced underground by the advance of Christianity. When my daughters were children, I desperately sought ways to celebrate our cultural holidays without being overtly Christian; I wanted them to value their Hindu heritage as well. Fortunately, I came across Edna Barth's series of holiday books that include *Holly, Reindeer, and Colored Lights*; *Lilies, Rabbits and Painted Eggs*; and *Witches, Pumpkins, and Grinning Ghosts* in which she explained the origins of each season's symbols. What a joy to discover, for example, that the custom of decorating an evergreen tree at the winter solstice went back as far as the Druids, my Celtic ancestors. And that the word *Easter* may have come from the Anglo-Saxon pre-Christian goddess of springtime and dawn called *Eostre*.

I find that I have an almost biological need to recognize and celebrate the changing of the seasons. It doesn't even matter whether there are children in the house or not. In fact, when I lived alone in a furnished, rented apartment for nine months a few years ago, the first thing I bought was not dishes, pans, or linens, but a live Christmas tree in a pot. It was August at the time, and every month I bought a glass ornament to symbolize my journey.

Name in writing a particular ritual custom you must carry out for a sense of connectedness to the universe. What do you feel compelled, from within, to do? Read aloud what you have written. ❧

FIFTEEN

RELATE A FICTIONAL LIFE

Relate: *to narrate or tell; to bring into logical association; to interact meaningfully*

PREPARING FOR AND CARRYING OUT the annual celebrations and traditions of the family is usually the responsibility of the women. It is out of women's sphere of home and hearth that have come the jokes, stories, customs, beliefs, songs, and legends of women's folklore, which differs greatly from men's. In fact, women's beliefs and value systems are so different that they often go unnoticed by the men.

This is shown beautifully in Susan Glaspell's play *Trifles*. An isolated farm wife has clearly murdered her husband by knotting a rope around his neck while he slept. But the sheriff and two other men can find no evidence to prove this, no matter how hard they search in the house and the barn. Meanwhile, the sheriff's wife and another woman, brought along to fetch some clothes for the woman being held in jail, are able to read such "trifling" details as dirty pans under the sink, burst jars of fruit, and erratically stitched quilt squares, and they piece together the motive for the murder. Because the men are so patronizing towards them in the story, the women close ranks to keep their information from the men (not difficult!) and protect the farm wife. The short-story version, which has just appeared in the "canon" of college reading lists, is called "A Jury of Her Peers."

Here is a piece of a legend I heard once while living at Fort Leavenworth, Kansas. A stone house on the post has been occupied by military families ever since it was built in the mid-nineteenth century. It is haunted. Apparently, a woman died alone in this house while her husband was away.

Select the number one, two, or three. If you are in a group, count off in threes. Ones, write about the woman. Who was she? Why was she in Kansas? What did she die of? Twos, write about the husband. Who was he, what was he doing in Kansas, and where was he while she was dying? Threes, write about how and why the house is haunted. Read aloud what you have written. Groups can read in sequences of three. ❧

SIXTEEN

REVISE A FAIRY TALE

Revise: *to change or modify*

MANY OF US GREW up hearing and reading fairy tales and internalizing the fantasy that the prince will come and save us and we will live happily ever after. Where did these fairy tales come from? The main themes seem to be a mixture of Celtic and Indian origin, which would help explain why more than 345 versions of "Cinderella" can be found between India and Ireland.

Some years ago, while studying Celtic mythology for a class, I came across a picture of a silver bracelet of Celtic origin, purportedly used for some socio-religious purpose rather than for ornamentation. It formed a circle ending in two cow heads facing one another. It is nearly identical to a silver bangle sent to my daughter by her Indian grandmother: a circle ending in two elephant heads facing one another.

Whatever the origin of the fairy tales, they all contain elements of enchantment, magic, wonder. I share with you my silver bangle. On difficult days it feels like a handcuff chaining me to the patriarchal expectations of my familial Ireland and my marital India. On more positive days, it's a symbol of the strong goddess tradition that predates the patriarchy in each of these cultures.

Today, many women poets are revising the old fairy tales to reflect what really happens after the princess goes off to live in the prince's kingdom. Marge Piercy's "Story Wet As Tears" about the frog prince is ironically funny; Maxine Kumin's "The Archaeology of a Marriage" about Sleeping Beauty fifty years later is sarcastically wistful; while Anne Sexton's book *Transformations* is outright chilling.

Go back to your favorite childhood fairy tale and write it out, revising it to reflect your life now. If you need some "magic" to help you move forward, I loan you my silver bangle. Read aloud what you have written. ✤

SEVENTEEN

REFORM A BIBLICAL STORY

Reform: *to improve, as by alteration; to form again*

OTHER STORIES THAT HAVE SHAPED US within our culture are to be found in the Bible. Whether we've been raised in the Judeo-Christian tradition or not, the metaphors, symbols, and images of the Bible live in our collective unconscious, and from there shape our lives without our always being aware of it. This is why my daughter found the Bible included on her college reading list for incoming freshman. To not know such biblical references as "the patience of Job" marks us as illiterate within our cultural context.

But what images do we, as women, internalize from the Bible? It is so clearly a book that is of, for, and by men. When we're included in it at all, it is in relationship to the male protagonists, as wives, mothers, sisters, daughters, whores. Our roles have been defined by the patriarchs and their male god.

Unlike the strong goddesses in the Hindu tradition of my inlaws or the Greek heritage I studied in sixth grade, few female figures in the Bible have any personalities or power of their own: All their energies are absorbed and utilized by the males, whether divine or human. We have, for instance, the Mother of God, but not God the Mother. The message that reverberates in our psyches is that feminine wisdom is of no account. We must play out our roles unquestioningly, in the image of meek and mild Mary, so that the begatting can continue. Mary pondered all things on the first Christmas Eve and kept them in her heart. What if someone had thought to ask her what she was thinking or feeling?

Rewrite a story from the Bible in which a woman appears, retelling it from her point of view. Read aloud what you have written. ❧

EIGHTEEN

REVERSE WOMAN'S SIN

Reverse: *to turn in the opposite direction, or order; to exchange positions of; to transpose*

SUPPOSE WE READ THE BIBLE as a metaphor of men's life journeys. For instance, what if the life, death, and resurrection of Jesus can be interpreted as a map to be followed, by men, towards wholeness? If the psychologists are right that a boy's task is to separate from his mother by developing strong ego boundaries, in order to be about his "father's business," then at mid-life the male's task is to "crucify" the ego that keeps him separated from his larger Self. Therefore, the selfishness we read about in the Bible is the "sin" that keeps *man* from becoming whole.

But what about women's life journeys? While separating from mother, the girl still retains a sense of identification with the source of her being; she is never totally cut off from the sacred within. But she is continually pitched away from this center, her place of wholeness, when she lives the way society says she should: through relationships with others, selflessly. Her mid-life task then becomes the opposite of the man's. She needs to develop ego boundaries that will help her redirect her energies inward, so that she may reawaken the Self of wholeness. Selflessness is *woman's* "sin."

This lack of a sense of self shows in many ways, as Valerie Saiving notes in her essay "The Human Situation" (in *Womanspirit Rising*): diffuseness, distractibility, dependence—yet instead of being encouraged to become a fully developed human being, a woman must deny her impulse towards wholeness if she would live out her role as defined by patriarchal religion and society.

Write about sin from a woman's perspective and experience. What cuts you off from your center and makes you feel scattered and unbalanced? For what do you need to be forgiven? What is your personal sin? Read aloud what you have written. ❧

NINETEEN

REALIZE THE UNIVERSAL

Realize: *to comprehend completely; to make real*

HOW DOES A WOMAN AWAKEN to the powers of being that connect her with the universe from within? In *Diving Deep and Surfacing,* Carol Christ suggests that the very sin of self-negation prepares a woman for the mystical experience of enlightenment/awakening. Her weak ego boundaries leave her more open to the mystic experience of union and integration with the powers of being. Christ goes on to note that mystical identification occurs for women in nature; a solitary walk in the woods can bring insights that assure her she is on her right "path," and reaffirm her selfhood. But mystical "aha!"s can also occur in community, especially in groups where women are empowering one another to name and value their experiences. Writing in a group, then sharing what's been written, reinforces this process.

Writing itself is a way to evoke mystical experience. Paying attention to the words you have put down on paper is akin to the mystic's concept of prayer as attention to God. It is no accident that mystics use metaphoric language to speak of that which can't be analyzed, only experienced. An inspired image, May Sarton tells us, is one that comes from below the surface of consciousness and points to what we really mean and know, not what we thought we knew.

Imagine a natural object, something as specific as a grain of sand, a mustard seed, a tree (rather than the whole forest). Let that "part" become a symbol for the whole that opens up the world and, as Eliade puts it, helps us attain the universal. If you can hear the truth it has to tell you through the words you use to name it, you may experience a oneness with your natural object and know its truth to be your own. Put your image into words and capture them in writing. Read aloud what you have written. ❧

RECLAIM THE MOON

Reclaim: *to make suitable for cultivation or habitation*

IT HAS LONG BEEN THOUGHT that women are closer to nature because of their biological cycles than men, who are always identified with culture. But that's no wonder: The culture we live in was created of, for, and by men. This is why many women find that they must go off to the woods or out in the garden for a place where, among insects, birds, and animals, they can be fully human. Is it possible that men created culture, beginning with initiation rites that emulated the natural blood-letting of women, as a way to exclude deliberately the women they were so jealous of?

Our patriarchal cultures continue to define and describe male life experience and to codify it in mythologies and religions. As Campbell reminds us, myths guide us, psychologically, through the stages of our lives. Psychology has finally verified what Hinduism has always known: Adults go through distinct phases of life that require differing tasks, tests, and responsibilities. Hinduism divides these stages into child, student, householder, and grandfather—when the man goes off into the forest for spiritual renewal. The woman goes with him, but it is his life and his journey. Even the custom of suttee, in which the widow burns herself alive on her husband's funeral pyre, was required so that she would ensure their passage into eternity together.

But where do we turn to find images and symbols and metaphors and myths reflecting women's life stages? Women have often been associated with the image of the moon: As the moon reflects the sun's light, so do women reflect back what isn't of their own power and making. The word *menstruation* itself comes from the monthly cycle of the moon.

Write about the moon. What does that image say of, for, or to you? How do you react to the sight of a full moon? Where were you and what were you doing (if you were alive) in July 1969 when a man landed on the moon? Read aloud what you have written. ❧

TWENTY ONE

REMEMBER MOTHERING

Remember: *to recall to the mind, think of again; to retain in the mind; to keep (someone) in mind*

THE WAXING, FULL, AND WANING phases of the moon have been represented in the image of the triple goddess: virgin, mother, and crone. Remember the fairy tale in which the queen longs for a daughter with skin white as snow, cheeks red as blood, and hair black as ebony? These are the goddess's colors: virgin—pure white, mother—blood red, and crone—wisdom black.

You have already written about your childhood, that time when you were a maiden, like Persephone out in the meadow picking wildflowers (and Heidi?), before the ground opened up under her. You may want to go back and reread what you wrote: it contains clues to the person you'll be called to become in the crone phase of your life.

But meanwhile, the mothering, full-bellied, full-moon phase demands that we set aside our needs and desires and our own self-identity in order to anticipate and meet the needs of the child who is totally dependent on us for survival. The home is our second womb that nurtures our children until they can be on their own. The responsibility is awesome, and unrewarded, except by lip service, in patriarchal societies. And so we shall celebrate it ourselves, for the ability (and willingness) to transcend our own thoughts and needs and interests in order to meet the needs of the child is an invaluable skill, as well as a profound experience. How many times did we wake up in the middle of the night before the child started crying? We know what we know, and do what we do, and it is good.

Name and value in writing an experience you've had nurturing others. Joseph Campbell remembers an old Chinese saying: Mothers are the only gods in whom all the world believes. Read aloud what you have written. ❧

TWENTY TWO

REJECT DISTRACTIONS

Reject: *to refuse to accept or grant; to discard, throw away*

THERE IS A GREAT DANGER of losing one's self completely during this nurturing phase; this is the place where selflessness becomes women's sin. I recall that, on the psychiatric ward where once I worked, the overwhelming majority of the patients were middle-aged, middle-class women, suffering from the empty nest syndrome. Drug and electroshock therapies did not seem to help long-term; these women were back on the unit, hospitalized with depression, again and again. Without someone else to live for and through, their lives lost all meaning. Yet, it is in this phase of life that a woman, finally finished with enabling others to live their lives, can fully become who she's meant to be. But how? And do we dare? After all, our Western patriarchal culture burned over eight million women at the stake over a three-hundred-year period of time because they claimed their power and used their wisdom.

Perhaps the image of the waning moon can be interpreted as the process of detaching and withdrawing into ourselves, so that our energy may go into giving birth to our Selves.

There is an old Chinese parable that says a man's task at mid-life is to go up the mountain and sit cross-legged, his hands on his thighs in the up position, saying yes to all the parts of himself he ignored, denied, or didn't develop while he was focusing on his career. But, the parable continues, a woman's task at mid-life is to go up the mountain and sit cross-legged, her hands on her thighs in the down position, putting her energy back into her own body and saying the great, creative *no* to all that has kept her pitched away from her center.

Write down what you will say the great "no" to. Or perhaps you need to say "yes" to some things in order to become more fully yourself. Read aloud what you have written. ❧

TWENTY THREE

REPOSE IN THE DARKNESS

Repose: *to lie at rest, relax; to place, as faith and trust in*

THERE IS ANOTHER PHASE of the moon: the fourth stage, that of total darkness. It can be seen metaphorically as the dark night of the soul, that never-never land where the old life has been lost or given up or outgrown and the new one hasn't fully emerged. The moon's three days dark is analogous to Christ's three days in the tomb. In many cultures, the moon is the place where souls go after death, to be judged and either sent on to heaven or sent back to earth in a new incarnation. This brings to mind the concept of purgatory, where one is cleansed of one's sins in order to be born into a new life. In any case, the moon can be viewed as a place of transformation; its darkness symbolizes fertility, inspiration, and immortality. As M. Ester Harding tells us in *Women's Mysteries*, the moon is the lesser light that rules the night of instinct and the inner, intuitive world within each of us.

As a writer, I find there's a dark night of the soul within the creative process. It is known as writer's block, and is a period of supreme frustration when a project one has been intensely involved with refuses to move forward. No matter how hard one tries, one cannot get from point A, the stage of preparation, to point E, the vaguely sensed end product. There is only one course of action, and that is to abandon the project: give up, give in, let it go; i.e., put it completely out of one's mind while one does something completely different. The problem then sinks down into another level of consciousness and remains there, brooding, simmering, working itself out, incubating, hibernating in that fertile, moon-dark, instinctive space.

Realizing that for many life is not a strictly linear journey, but a series of cycles (like the moon?) that spiral backwards to rework unresolved issues before moving forward, what experience(s) of the dark night of the soul have you had? Or, how do you imagine it to be? Write about your experiences or thoughts. Read aloud what you have written. ❧

TWENTY FOUR

RESPOND TO ANIMATION

Respond: *to react positively*

WHO OR WHAT WILL SAVE YOU from the dark night of the soul, rescue you from the abyss, carry you into the new life? In ancient cultures, the savior figures were female: Isis, Ishtar, Inanna. And there are surviving Irish folk tales in which the female voluntarily descends into hell to rescue the male. This makes sense on a psychological level. The soul has always been recognized as feminine, even in patriarchal religions; for the male to be psychologically whole he must be in relationship with the feminine within his own psyche. Jung named this the anima: she is man's *in*spiration, the muse guiding his creation.

But what of the woman experiencing the dark night of the soul? Because she *is* female, she is one with the mysterious source of her being, but she doesn't always know, feel, or believe it. The male part of her psyche, the animus, is not her inspiration. As Irene Claremont de Castillejo explains in *Knowing Woman*, the animus' task is merely to show the woman what is already there, within herself. When she has been pitched away from her center and lost in the abyss, the animus is the spirit that fans the dying embers back to life in her being. He is not the goal of the journey she must make to be whole; rather, he is a Hermes figure standing at the crossroads, showing her the

47

direction in which she must go, alone. If she stops to make a relationship with him, she will not get to where she's meant to go.

We women usually become aware of the animus figure within our psyches when we project it onto a real person in our lives. We suddenly find ourselves irrationally attracted to someone we are not, can not, should not be married to. He or she becomes what John Sanford calls "the invisible partner" in our lives; we obsess, fantasize, and dream about that person almost against our will.

Describe in writing the person you fantasize about, the one who so stirs you up that he or she awakens parts of you that you thought/felt were long dead, the one who animates your being, your animus. Read aloud what you have written. ❧

TWENTY FIVE

RE-CREATE YOURSELF

Re-create: *to create anew*

THERE IS A TERRIBLE DANGER of being "carried away" by the projected animus figure, and again distracted from our goal: reaching that place deep within where we are again whole. Any "marriage" with the animus figure must take place within the psyche, not out in the real world. Only then can the journey towards transformation continue. The marriage within the psyche produces the Divine Child: the spiritual self. For the woman the goal is to become "virgin" again, just as the new moon is reborn from the darkness. The word *virgin* here refers to its original meaning: spiritual (not biological) intactness. To become virgin again means a woman becomes "one-in-herself."

This parallels the creative process I began discussing earlier. The attraction to, union with, and fertilization by the animus figure within the woman's psyche leads to that time of incubation within that moon-dark place below the level of consciousness. In its own time (just like a real baby!) the solution to the creative problem reveals itself, most often when you least expect it, such as in the middle of the night. This illumination (the moon's light?), with continued hard work, can bring forth something altogether new: a poem, a book, an invention, a scientific theory, a social action.

Metaphorically, the process feels like Persephone's return from the underworld to be reunited with her mother, so the earth will burst forth from winter into spring. It's the sheer magic, wonder, and surprise of that first spring flower you see.

Name and develop in writing your metaphor for rebirth, reincarnation, renewal, resurrection. Read aloud what you have written. ❧

TWENTY SIX

REVEAL HEAVEN HERE AND NOW

Reveal: *to make known*

WE EXPERIENCE GLIMPSES of the "new" self that is possible during moments of at-one-ment, inner peace, profound joy, or even the wonder of going outside again after being stuck in the house with the flu, ill ourselves and/or nursing sick family members. Everything looks suddenly different: fresh and new. We see things we hadn't noticed or appreciated before. They were there all the time, but something had to happen within us before we could truly see. This brings to mind the Gnostic Gospel according to Thomas in which Jesus promises us that the kingdom of heaven is spread upon the earth if we would but see it. In other words, the eternal, the no where, is really now here: it just depends on your perspective, or where you place the "w."

In his final book, *The Inner Reaches of Outer Space: Metaphor as Myth and as Religion*, Joseph Campbell assures us we can live in both the eternal and temporal worlds simultaneously through metaphor: The symbols of the sacred interpreted poetically and psychologically, rather than literally, give us a sense of actual participation in the Infinite, the Transcendent. In short, a metaphor, because it implies a relationship between two differing things, changes our comprehension of them both. It begins with something concrete and carries it outward, to new and unpredictable places. The surprise at the other end comes as an "aha!," a revelation that transcends the individual personality.

Try to find and write about a metaphor that names how you feel when you experience your "new" self. In other words, what is your image of heaven, paradise, the Garden of Eden? How does the world look and feel when you are centered, at one with yourself? Read aloud what you have written. ❧

TWENTY SEVEN

RESIST HELL'S TRAPPINGS

Resist: *to strive or work against; to withstand*

OF COURSE YOU KNOW what's coming next: there's no way we can speak metaphorically of heaven without also naming our personal metaphors for hell.

Hell is often depicted in comics as a place red with flames. For me, flaming red symbolizes anger, my personal experience of hell. I get trapped in anger when I feel invisible, unvalued, and taken for granted or taken advantage of. I become angry when I feel my "new" self being sucked back into old, untransformed behavior that keeps me in the role of victim, i.e., being acted upon rather than taking positive action. And I fly into an absolute rage whenever I come across yet another example of how my society subtly undermines women's positive self-image.

For example, a March for Women's Lives in Washington, DC, drew well over the estimated half a million people. At least ninety percent of us were females. Yet, when the local paper reported the event, it led off with a quote from a white, middle-class, middle-aged male saying the march was a good thing and that the political leaders of the country ought to take notice. This particular male is a church member friend whom I admire and agree with. But from my perspective as a feminist, I interpret the media's quoting him as needing a (white) male to legitimize women's rights, issues, and concerns. And this infuriates me. But if I express my anger, I'll be perceived as a castrating bitch/witch who ought to be grateful that men marched in support of women at all and that the paper even bothered to report the event. Instead, I'm resentful. I identify with Kali, Hindu goddess of destruction, often depicted as a hideous hag, dancing on her husband's corpse, devouring his entrails.

Explore your personal metaphor for hell. You don't have to act it out; write it instead. Read aloud what you have written. ✺

TWENTY EIGHT

RETURN TO DO WHAT

Return: *to come back; to respond*

NOW WHAT? Do you stay stuck in your hell, or do you learn what it's trying to teach you and move on? Kali's destructiveness is for a purpose: to break down the old and make way for the new. But often, as women, we internalize our hell, blame ourselves for our pain, and thereby reinforce our powerlessness to live the lives we are meant to live.

This is even reflected in our literature. In *Archetypal Patterns in Women's Fiction*, Annis Pratt notes that spiritual journeys that give birth to strong, powerful, autonomous, transformed women often end in punishment, rather than reward. Women are more than likely driven mad or to suicide when they try to reintegrate themselves into society. Society simply isn't ready to receive the woman who returns from the mountaintop with her dream.

So, do we give up and give in—or change society so that we can live out full, meaningful lives? Why shouldn't society reflect our values and meet our needs: We make up more than half of it! Yet everything in it—from the personal (family structures) to the political (the structures of government, religion, the economy, even the legal system)—is constructed around the needs and values of men, *as if their perspectives were the whole picture.* I remember when I was working on my Peace Studies degree. I was an army wife at the time, and the commander took me aside at a party and told me how much he admired what I was doing but went on to assure me that "war is simply a part of human nature." I didn't know then, but do know now, that I should have replied, "Speak for yourself!"

Name in writing something you would change in your world so you would feel at home in it. Let your imagination go. And why not? If we don't have a vision to work towards, we will never begin the process of moving forward. We will stay stuck in hell. Read aloud what you have written. ❧

TWENTY NINE

REQUIRE CHANGES

Require: *to need; to demand, insist upon*

ONE WAY TO BEGIN MAKING CHANGES in the outside world is to accept, honor, and value what we need as women. Until and unless we take ourselves seriously, "they" won't, either. Becoming "one of the boys" and playing by their rules changes nothing; it just makes us complicit in maintaining the status quo. Instead, we must listen to our inner voices when we find ourselves uncomfortable in male-constructed situations. What does it mean if we find ourselves anxious, upset, or depressed in roles that seem so natural for men? Perhaps they're not so natural for women.

For example, I was acutely aware of being almost physically ill whenever I walked into a university classroom to teach. I didn't have all the answers to anything, only a little more knowledge and experience than (most of) my students. Yet they looked up to me as a voice of authority. I always felt like a fraud; I described my teaching style as "bluffing." My male colleagues assured me that everyone feels that way. Everyone is, in fact, bluffing, all the way to the top of the hierarchy. (Now there's a scary thought!) Mercifully, I came across Peggy McIntosh's article, "Feeling Like Fraud," in which she assured me that my discomfort came from being put in a hierarchical role. As a woman, I long ago internalized that I don't deserve to be in a position of authority: the majority of people I've observed at the top of anything have been men. Women don't belong there. Plus, women don't *like* being there. It's not so much that women *can't* stand behind podiums, McIntosh tells us, as that we women can't *stand* podiums!

And yet now I reach out (i.e., preach) from my life experience and invite congregants into their own inner and intra-personal spiritual work. I have gone from barely surviving at a podium to thriving in the pulpit. What's the difference? Perhaps only this: When I wasn't in touch with and honoring the truth of my own life, I *was* a fraud. Now that I have learned to live out of my authentic Self, I am filled with a joyful sense of freedom and inward peace, out of which I am empowered to do the life work I am meant to be doing.

Identify something required of you in our patriarchal society that makes you uncomfortable. Examine it in writing. Accept your discomfort as a clue to what could and should be changed, both outside and within yourself. Read aloud what you have written. ❧

THIRTY

REJOICE IN A GLIMPSE OF THE MYSTERY

Rejoice: *to feel or be joy-full*

ONE BEGINS GRADUALLY TO GET A GLIMPSE of what it is like to live out of the center of one's full self. The closest word for this experience is *freedom*. The sense of infinite possibilities that opens up reveals heaven as the positive energy released when you are free to be wholly your Holy Self. You are happy and joyful and free.

Once you have that experience, you begin to yearn for it more and more. The *I* (firsthand) experience becomes as an *eye* into the Great Mystery of the universe that some choose to call God. And once you have even a brief experience of freedom, wholeness, and the presence of the Holy, you'll want to keep moving towards that center, that "eye."

We begin to recognize the ways we cut ourselves off from that place, the behaviors through which we pitch ourselves away from our centers, causing us to *miss the mark* (the original definition of sin). Also, as we commit to moving more and more into that experience of the Holy, other people in our lives who are not on a similar path will try, overtly and/or covertly, to block us (my definition of evil). This can set up the counteracting experience of fear: the fear of our own possibilities that shuts us down again within our own self-limitations and keeps us stuck there.

Ministry has been broadly defined as the intersection between your spiritual gifts (yes, *your* gifts) and what needs doing in the wider world, the very thing that won't get done unless *you* do it. So the call to ministry becomes first and foremost a call to freedom and fullness of being. Once we give in to that call, we can no longer participate in that which oppresses the sense of the Mystery within us. But our passion must be rooted in our glimpse of the Great Mystery.

Write about an experience you have had with freedom. When you hear that word, what do you see, hear, taste, touch, feel, imagine, anticipate, remember, or long for? Read aloud what you have written. ❧

THIRTY ONE

RESPOND TO THE CALL

Respond: *to reply, to answer*

ONCE YOU HAVE TAPPED into your experience of the Great Mystery, a yearning for it develops that demands your attention. A dialogue gets set into motion, a dialogue of call and response, call and response. You start listening, you start hearing, and you start responding. This call and response goes on for years, and with response comes response-ability.

Your glimpses of freedom invite you to become your authentic self, so that the Mystery can be fully present through all that you do.

For men, surrender to the Mystery means saying a great Yes, as can be seen in the lives of Jesus, Buddha, Lao Tse, Gandhi, Rumi.

This surrender for a woman is the freedom to speak her truth with clarity. Male theologians are beginning to use the image of the woman and child coming in from the desert to describe the return of feminine wisdom. Thus we adult women are said to be brokering in the new spiritual age. However, we women have within our collective psyches the image of countless other women being burned at the stake for their truth. And so we are wary of bringing our truth to the table of theological discourse.

Yet by not naming our truth we betray the Great Mystery.

Women have been silent and silenced for so long that before we dare bring our truth out into the general discussion, we must first witness to/be witnessed by other women. In fact, because we women are relational in our way of being in the world, women theologians and therapists, spiritual directors and pastors are discovering and encouraging women doing their deep inner work to do so in small, safe group settings.

As our inner truth emerges, another person can not only reflect back what was heard, but can hold us accountable to and for it. We thus take responsibility for what we know. Also, as we hear another's truth, we often hear a piece of our own truth that we haven't been able to be in touch with or articulate as yet. Thus the Great Mystery emerges through many voices and experiences.

Write about a previously silent/silenced piece of your truth that you can begin to grasp as a faithful glimpse into the Mystery. Read aloud what you have written. ❧

THIRTY TWO

REFUSE TO GO BACK

Refuse: *to decline to do, accept, allow, or give*

SYSTEMS THEORY TEACHES us that as we try to change, both the private and public spheres of our lives will conspire to pull us back into the old familiar patterns of behavior, for the sake of the homeostasis of the status quo. As in the ancient stories of death threats made against the newborn (Moses, Jesus, various fairy tales), we must be wary and constantly on guard. This is often the biggest challenge that women find in following their spiritual path. Quite often this manifests first in our dreams, not unlike the story of Joseph being instructed in a dream to flee to Egypt with the new mother and holy child.

As was noted before, all dreams come in the service of health and wholeness. This includes even the nightmares—especially the nightmares: They really want us to pay attention to something important. In the dream group I participated in for two years while doing this inner work, every one of us had our "911 nightmares," dreams in which we were trapped inside burning or collapsing or flooding buildings and were calling for outside help, all to no avail. But any 911 call that is not responded to in a dream is usually a sign that the dreamer needs to take responsibility for dealing with whatever is posing a threat.

This brings to mind the definition of *conversion* I learned in a class on Liberation Theology as "the conscious decision to take responsibility for subsequent development in one or more of these areas of one's life: psychological, emotional, moral, socio-political, spiritual." The key word here is "conscious." For to default on making a decision by ignoring the issue is also making a choice.

Of course the results may not be as dramatic or as definitive as putting out a fire or clobbering a demon in a dream. Rather, by making even a small change in attitude, one sets into motion a chain reaction that affects norms, habits, behaviors, and values that then feed into the new experience (nurture and nourish the new being). But it all begins, not with having a blueprint for how things are expected to turn out, but with simply acting on and taking responsibility for the new and saying no to whatever threatens to swallow you back into the old.

From what part of yourself might the new need protection? Explore your answer in writing. Read aloud what you have written. ✺

THIRTY THREE

REMAIN IN LIMINAL SPACE

Remain: *to endure or persist*

THIS IS THE "OHMYGODWHATHAVEIDONE" PHASE of spiritual journeying, when the old has ceased to be and the new hasn't fully materialized. This is the liminal time, the threshold between two realities, a wilderness time, the time for wandering around in the desert, disoriented, murmuring, bewildered, fearful of a willful return to what was enslaving because at least that is comfortably familiar.

Often it is companion wanderers who keep us moving forward. In his classic *Walking*, Henry David Thoreau informs us that the word *sauntering* comes "from idle people who roved about the country, in the Middle Ages, and asked charity, under the pretense of going à la Sainte Terre, to the Holy Land, till the children explained, 'There goes a Sainte-Terrer,' a Saunterer—a Holy-Lander." Thoreau goes on to claim that "every walk is a sort of a crusade, preached by some Peter the Hermit within us, to go forth and reconquer this Holy Land from the hands of the [inner] Infidels."

But we don't have to go it alone. We find the fellow pilgrims with whom we can be totally honest, those to whom we can entrust our deepest truths, those who will help hold our stories because they can accept us for who we are. These are the precious ones who come to believe us and believe in us, who bear witness to what we have done and what was done to us, as well as what we hope for, think about, and feel.

As Jean Shinoda Bolen notes in *Crossing to Avalon*, it is no small matter to be a witness to another person's life story. By listening with compassion, we validate each other's lives, make suffering meaningful, and help the process of forgiving and healing to take place. But this can only happen among people who have no vested interest in keeping you from growing/going forward.

Identify and celebrate in writing the pilgrims sharing your journey, those people who are helping you persevere in the liminal space. Describe how it sometimes seems the great powers of the universe have put these people in your life for precisely this purpose. Read aloud what you have written. ❧

THIRTY FOUR

RECEIVE AFFIRMATION

Receive: *to greet or welcome*

HOW DO WE KNOW we are on the right path during this liminal, wilderness time? Little synchronicities appear, what Carl Jung calls "meaningful coincidences." Something happens in the outer world that connects with your inner journey and produces an "aha!" This comes about because we are indeed part of the interconnected web of the universe, and it has to do with energy flow and intent and paying attention.

Hints and hunches come to us daily, but many are so brief and so small that we miss them or deem them to be inconsequential. Yet these are the very ways that the universe sends us messages of affirmation and tells us, through insight and impulse and inclination, what's to be done next, one small step at a time.

For an intuitive instant, you suddenly experience a deep sense of knowing that you are one with the universe, and that, just like a plant's self-fulfillment of moving naturally from seed to primary leaves to secondary leaves to stem to blossom to seed, you too are unfolding into what you are meant to become.

This can be experienced as a covenant, a commitment, a promise to and with and from the powers of Being within the universe.

Describe in writing any little synchronicities that have appeared along your path—secret messages in a bottle meant only for you. Read aloud what you have written. ❧

THIRTY FIVE

REFRAME YOUR LIFE STORY

Reframe: *to reconstruct, rebuild, redesign*

WHEN WE WOMEN SPEAK OUR TRUTH out of our newly found authentic selves, we do not pronounce it as normative, i.e., a universal truth that all should aspire to. Rather, we describe it through narrative, using the story of our own lives to offer a truth others may, or may not, identify with.

Our scripted lives can become our sacred scripture: the material on which to reflect, make meaning, and do theology. This is important in a woman's spiritual journey because the accompanying feelings of regret and guilt over what, or who, had to be left behind can be overwhelming. But in time and with patience, there can come a point when grace breaks through the layers of grief, and we can stop looking back and seeing what we could/should/would have tried harder to fix and finally accept that things were not to be fixed after all. We can begin to see within the painful story of "what went wrong," the accumulating evidence of the movement of the spirit within our lives.

This shift in perspective begins with looking back in gratitude. For at the bottom of the great well of grief lies grace, *gracias*, gratefulness for the journey. Giving thanks has been said to be the only true form of prayer. This is because when you open your heart and mind and soul in gratitude for all that is your life, there is simply no room left for grief and regret, self-doubt and self-destructive behaviors, anger and blaming. Instead there is only a profound sense of the presence of grace.

Begin a written list of things you are grateful for within your own life story. Read aloud what you have written. Doing this on a daily basis can keep this channel of grace open to you. ❧

THIRTY SIX

RECALL A HISTORICAL WOMAN

Recall: *to call back, ask or order to return; to remember*

WHERE DO WE LOOK for stories of self-actualized women leading authentic, valued lives in which we can see our own struggles reflected? Certainly, you may have noticed, not in our history books. Many years ago, a writing mentor recommended that I read Hendrik Van Loon's *The Story of Mankind* and study his use of language: the book had won the first Newbery Medal awarded for excellence in children's books. I was depressed for days after reading it. It was a narrative of continuous warfare. What a tragic commentary on human history! Now, many years later, I finally realize it was only a partial history: the story of *man*kind, white, Western *man*kind.

What were the women doing throughout the thousands of years of (male) recorded history? Elise Boulding sets out to explore this in her monumental *The Underside of History: A View of Women Through Time*. For without a past, we have no present, much less a future: We do not see ourselves as participants in the human experience! One of the biggest "aha!"s for me in Elise's book was reading that the suffrage movement came about because women, who were trying to deal with the negative social impact of increasing industrialization, suddenly realized they needed access to political power in order to effect change. For centuries women have carried the moral values of society, but in order to fully carry them out, women need to be out in the public sphere rather than stuck on a pedestal and sentimentalized for our "superior" natures while treated as inferior members of society. The suffragists not only won the vote for us, they got us into the history books, if only a line that mentions that in 1920, men "gave" us the vote. An alternate book I use with Peace Studies students, *The Power of the People: Active Nonviolence in the United States* (300 years of "hidden" history!), includes a picture of a suffragist being force-fed at Lorton Prison.

Can we bring women from history forward into our own lives to serve as mentors and friends? Is there a woman in history with whom you have an affinity? Write about some connections between your lives, honoring you both. Read aloud what you have written. ✤

THIRTY SEVEN

RECONCILE YOUR WORLDVIEW

Reconcile: *to make compatible or consistent*

AFTER NEARLY FIFTY YEARS of struggling for women's right to vote, Elizabeth Cady Stanton called together a committee of thirty women scholars to reevaluate the passages of the Bible that either referred to women or excluded women. She had come to realize that the sexist language, symbols, and stories in the Bible were being used to reinforce and legitimize men's determination to keep women in an inferior position in society. Stanton and her scholars dared to believe that sexism existed in the Bible because it had been interpreted by men: fallible men. For example, when they went back to the original Hebrew word for creator they found it was not *Yahweh*, but *Elohim*, a plural word that can refer to either male or female god or gods. The result of their work, published in 1895, is known as *The Woman's Bible*.

Women in religion today, over a hundred years later, have made great progress in having inclusive language used in church liturgy, hymns, and biblical readings. But merely including the feminine pronoun in front of male terms such as power, glory, dominion, judge, ruler, kingdom, omnipotent, everlasting, almighty, etc., leaves me as alienated as ever. Would the Old Testament read like such a war epic, with the Hebrews forever putting everything

73

"to the sword" as commanded by Yahweh, if, in the beginning, the creator had truly been equally female?

The great mother goddess of pre-patriarchal times created everything out of her own body, rather than standing outside of creation, one step removed, saying "Let there be . . . ." She was in the world, and of it, as it was of her.

Write a creation story out of the feminine matrix, your worldview perspective as a woman. Read aloud what you have written. ❧

THIRTY EIGHT

REREAD WOMEN'S LITERATURE

Reread: *to read again*

ONE WAY TO CONNECT your story with the larger story of women everywhere is by reading what they've written about spirituality. Until recently, however, there has been no sacred text, such as the Bible, the Koran, the Bhagavad Gita, the Tao de Ching, or the Talmud, in which to find specifically women's spiritual journeys. Rather, we must look to women's literature, especially poetry.

For example, in her 1994 book *Women in Praise of the Sacred*, Jane Hirshfield presents forty-three centuries of spiritual poetry by women. From Asia and Africa and the Middle East and Europe and America come the voices of women describing their spiritual experiences.

But to be able to read other writers for their inspiration takes a different mindset than the one we developed in school: We are not to compare and contrast, dispute, discern, or debate the material at hand. Instead, we must learn to sit with it in an attitude of prayerful meditation, open to receiving new insights they may hold (for "lustres," as Emerson called them). As Thoreau explained in *Walden*: "To read well, that is to read true books in a true spirit, is a noble exercise. Books must be read as deliberately as they were written."

How exactly might we do that? Here are four ways:

Embrace the whole picture.
Open to the empty space between the lines.
Envision other possibilities.
Authenticate what changes or confirms you.

Use the four ways described above to read and reread the following words of Emily Dickinson.

> *The Infinite a sudden Guest*
> *Has been assumed to be—*
> *But how can that stupendous come*
> *Which never went away?*

Then write down whatever insights and "aha!"s come to you. For example, my insight here is that I've always believed we can only experience the infinite in brief glimpses, like a sudden guest arriving from somewhere else. Yet clearly, the infinite is always in our midst, and we simply don't realize it. Read aloud what you have written. ❧

THIRTY NINE

RESTORE YOUR IMAGE OF THE SACRED

Restore: *to bring back into existence or use*

ELISE BOULDING WRITES in *The Underside of History* that because
every society develops its own symbols to support its view of the
cosmos and the place of people within it, patriarchal cultures build
subordinate images of women into the cosmologies and creation
stories, and then rationalize their treatment of women accordingly.
Men's dualistic viewpoint of women as "other" keeps us out of the
mainstream of God-the-Father–sanctioned political (i.e., public
sphere) power; we are out in the margins along with all the "others": children, slaves, men of color, etc. Meanwhile, the cosmology
that gives *man* dominion over all the earth now threatens to de-
stroy the planet economically, environmentally, militarily, and spir-
itually. We desperately need the balance of the feminine
perspective if we are to survive as a species.

The divine feminine wisdom that was swallowed by the patriarchy 5,000 years ago is re-emerging today, calling us to affirm
what we as women intuitively know: that all life is interconnected and sacred. But this only happens as we women speak up
for our values and visions, in both the private and the public
spheres. Only as we begin to question men's definitions of right
and wrong, as Carol Gilligan does in *In a Different Voice*, will we be

able to rename, redefine, recreate, revise (see again) the world as it can be.

Women studying religion have come to realize that a theologian's gender has a lot to do with her/his theological conclusions. And they have come to the conclusion that the first principle of theology "done" from a woman's perspective is the personal experience of the sacred. Unlike male theologians who name God as separate from themselves, just as they separated from mother in childhood, women theologians retain a sense of oneness with the source of their being. Therefore, their experience of the Divine/Ultimate/Sacred differs from male experience.

Write about a word, image, symbol, or metaphor that names the sacred for you. Read aloud what you have written. ❧

FORTY

RESHAPE YOUR OWN NAMING

Reshape: *to give new form to; to develop*

NOW, HOW TO KEEP GOING? Before you are tempted to say that you have nothing else to write about, let me say "nonsense!" You've barely begun. If you look back over all you've written in response to the suggested exercises, you'll find you've got a body of work to continue with. Eight to ten minutes is barely enough time to get something started. You can go back to each of your writings and revise it, see it again. But one word of advice: Please don't discard any of the versions you do of a work, especially the original. Your final revision may say something very different from what your first draft wanted to say; you may need or want to go back to the original impulse.

There are several techniques you can use to open up what's already been written, to reveal new insights or deepen what's already there. You can expand a piece by playing with strong words within it and letting them open up into images and symbols larger than you thought you intended. You can condense a piece by taking out weak words (like adjectives) and thereby making the whole tighter and stronger. You can rearrange lines to let them play off one another in new ways. You can go back to a strong phrase that people responded to (with gasps, "aha!"s, or giggles) and begin a new piece with that as a first line. You can repeat lines like a chant or an echo, and polish your lines so they have a rhythmic sound. You can substitute words that play off one another alliteratively.

You can continue reading your work aloud, for affirmation, feedback, and a sense of rightness of its sound to yourself, as well as to others. The women at my church have used their writing as the basis for women's worship services. Not only did they hear their own experiences and insights valued, but they evoked other women's celebration of their own insights and experiences.

For a final exercise here, and the beginning of your continuing effort, retrieve a piece you have already written and begin to revise it. Use line breaks and stanza spacing to set off key images and insights so you experience them in a new, perhaps more intense, way. Read aloud what you have written. ❧

CONCLUSION

THE IDEA FOR DEVELOPING these exercises began in 1985, when I attended a retreat on women and religion. Nearly every woman there admitted she had written at some time or other in her life. This makes sense, of course, because writing needs no expensive equipment or special training; the tools are readily at hand, and one can always find a little time to scribble standing in line at the market or when the family is sleeping. Yet nearly every woman there also admitted she'd never shared what she'd written with anyone but rather had hidden it away in some drawer. These exercises offer the opportunity to break away from this self-imposed secrecy. If you have done these exercises in a group, you've already shared your truth. If you have done these exercises alone, you are continuing the tradition of diary, journal, and letter writing that has been the source of our knowledge about women's lives throughout recorded history. Will you continue? Will you choose to promote your vision and values through your word and your actions? Treasure your own insights as you approach that reality.

WRITING SAMPLES

❧ ONE

Joan Starr in transition again.
Mother with a vengeance.
Passionate teacher.
Emotional, intuitive, mystic.
Rather typical for my time and place.
Brooklyn born and energized in big-city international culture.
Word lover, reverence for written words and pages.
Stories are cherished companions and memories are stored
    from questing journeys.

Joan Starr

Name: Ada from my grandmother and Katherine from my other grandmother, something I hated as a girl but now regard as a nice way to be tied in with my beginnings.

Height: too much, once, I felt awkward, gangly, somehow or other my arms and legs never went in manageable directions. Now, it's nice to be tall, able to see above some parts of the crowd, able to wear "tall people" clothes.

Age: getting older, for which I am grateful, and with added years is coming a sense of mellowness that is new and easier to live with than the obligations of my youth.

Eyes: grey to blue to green depending on what I wear, the weather, my mood—real barometers of the situation I am in.

Ada Churchill

TWO

I am the oak that never sheds its leaves
for I've known no dormant seasons.
My roots have found their way deep into
the earth. They anchor me as their
invisible tentacles suck nutrients for my soul.
My branches stretch to the warm sunshine.
At times they grow to a space where I am
not wanted. They cut me back. I become
crooked, unbalanced. And then, from the wound,
I grow new buds, to twigs, to branches
reaching once again for the sunshine.
I have good growing seasons.
But have also suffered blight.
Many times and for many years
I've been the host to other living
creatures. Some grateful for my nurturing.
Some wanting only to suck my juices dry
and leave me hollow. And yet I stand just the same—
but forever changing.

                                        Miriam Phoebe Newton

I have flown as a butterfly
Soared as a hawk
Played at being a mirror
Reflecting surfaces,
Coiled snake-like forming a circle

Mouth to tail.
Now, I am a web-spinner
Trying to leave patterns
To mark the places I have been.
To leave a trace, a mark that I was here
To share with those to come a hint
Of what the journey has been like
I'm seeking a thread with tensile strength
To keep my fragile lacelike work
From disappearing before it's read.

Joan Starr

꙳ THREE

It is spring again. The columbine in the front yard is beginning to bloom again. I watch intensely, looking forward to the return of the deep pink blossoms that kept me company on my windowsill the previous spring. But when the lone blossom finally raises its head, it is vivid red, with a bright yellow center!

I am stunned and mystified. The gardener explains that the columbine sold by nurseries are cultivars: They have been cultivated to produce their various colored, showy large blossoms. The small red and yellow blossom we are looking at is just like the wild columbine I've seen growing along the ocean bluffs.

In fact, the cultivated columbine has reverted to its original state of being; it has become its essential self.

As I too was becoming, in seminary.

Gail Collins-Ranadive

FOUR

All the other trees grow up leafy green and full, but what is this?
Thorny and dark, maybe this isn't a tree at all. Is it alive? Well, yes, it
appears to be. It has lasted all these years, right alongside the tall trees.
Too bad it can't pull itself together like the others. Oddly, this strange
plant regularly produces shiny red berries that ripen into yellow flow-
ers. If it weren't for those berries, we wouldn't even know it was alive.

Susan Holst

❧ FIVE

In the Beginning
and I am washing, ironing, rehanging perma-press
curtains, before spring classes begin
always before I've done this to silence
the voice of my mother in the back of my mind
I know now
there's no voice,
just the act:
Barbara scouring bathrooms
two days before surgery
Peggy scrubbing the floor
on the day she left her husband
Mother eight months pregnant with a seventh child
cleaning the corners of upstairs windows with a toothbrush
why this propitiation?
ask Marsha why she made the beds
before driving the wrong way down the highway.

Gail Collins-Ranadive

Perhaps the tree I knew most intimately was the one that bore apples every summer during my third to tenth years. My sister Cathy and I would climb that tree, sprawl out on its smooth, curved limbs, wrap our silky legs around its hard core. We would pick the apples, eat a few, but most were transformed into Mother's succulent apple pies. The apple tree was home, a play place, a nest for squirrel-like girls in their early years.

Years later it was another tree that helped me choose Cathy's grave—a graceful, towery eucalyptus, its leaves like tiny flags waving against a deep blue California sky. Beneath that tree we laid my sister's body to rest—and it is thus that I know trees to be sentinels of life, and death. In the case of the eucalyptus, that tree helps me know Cathy lives on forever—in the tree's roots and branches, in the wind that dances through its leaves, and in my heart.

Carolyn Cottom

If there is an afterlife, may I become a tree—magnificent, reliable, asymmetrical, growing, changing, essentially there—always predictable, and welcoming, enveloping, and free.

If I could paint it would be trees. Sentinels of the earth, my own Lord of the Heavens. Elegant asymmetry unfolding endlessly without restraint, without warning, impulsively, playfully, and mysteriously—one branch into another into another until adorned by leaves or seasonal bouquets.

Jeanne Gayler

SEVEN

Suddenly I am crouched in a small enclosure and there are dead fish lying on the floor, or is it the ground? These fish are terrible to look at, meaning something awful has happened. The fish open up, as if sliced in half. I poke my head outside to see if it is safe. I cannot tell, so I wait there.

Karen Bennett

EIGHT

A snake gently twists across
the sloping desert
    tracing
the passionate spirals
and undulations of women's
curves on the swelling sand.
    The silent wind creeps
behind
    erasing our serpentine
forms with dusty breaths.
A desert enigma of lost journeys,
and hidden hieroglyphs
as infinite as sand,
    as infinite as women's words.

Katherine Bartov

❧ NINE

Everyone else looks great, lots of pastel linen suits. Of course they stay clear of me, though they know me well. Sometimes I wonder why I don't dress up like they do. Even with my snake body, some linen might bring out the girl in me. I guess I can't be bothered. Needless to say, without any arms, I'm not wearing gloves. And when they serve the tea, I just fling my scaly tail across the divan and dip my long tongue into the cup. Delicious. I'm done before the others have even started.

Susan Holst

❧ TEN

On the Eve
of the equinox
first menses calls
a young daughter
out of childhood,
the moon sheds its shadow
the serpent its skin
and Eve is expelled
from the Garden
again.
Rites of passage
for this generation
take place on the track
a baton passed on in a race

her team sister gives
her a rose the same shade
of the stain on her sheets:
this "messiness"
connects her with
the Eastern-block athletes
at the Munich Olympics
besieging the doctor
for whole boxes of pads
then the hostages taken
no way to save them
but to try cyanide
shot in by canister
if all dropped simultaneously
Herr Doktor could
rush in, revive
with his antidote, his life's
research proved
if not
the headlines would
read "German Doctor
Gasses Jews
Again" instead
in a splatter of blood
the Israelis pass
back into the Garden.
Now this daughter
dreams the Olympics
and, with the startle
of blood, of becoming
a mother.

Gail Collins-Ranadive

Images of raucous wonderful birthday parties from pictures and eight mm movies made by my Uncle Bill show a child with a blazing aura, and tons of energy. I taught neighborhood kids how to ride bikes; I raced, swung from ropes over the water, flew across the frozen bay in winter—on skates, holding a sheet—rode on ice boats, crewed on sailboats, climbed up on the roof of my parents' house, down trees—all wildness, and then it all began to change for me by about the eighth grade.

Cassie Arnold

Damned if I'd sit in Mama's parlor and eat those goddamned little, white-bread sandwiches with the crusts all cut off, or make rainbow-colored jello-molds to pass around to the ladies, who plucked their eyebrows to look like Tallulah Bankhead! Off I'd go to climb my tree with a bag of green plums and the latest sex novel I'd snitched from under my aunt's bed. Safe— set astride those limbs. High, high above the gushy, asinine silliness—lovely, sinful delicious feeling of superiority. Alone, away from the babble and the trivia. I knew what would happen if I got caught and dragged out to be paraded around, with all the ladies exclaiming: "Oh, look at her big brown eyes"—the hives, that's what would happen: fat, fiery, itchy welts, my own body physically announcing its rebellion. Every corpuscle saying *no*!

Jeanne Gayler

TWELVE

It begins when you're made to clean up your plate because
people are starving in _____ fill in the blank. For me, it was India.
From then on, you're haunted. Gaunt possibilities squat on
emaciated legs; dark eyes stare at those grains of rice
you are wasting. Their village stands in perpetual drought: land's
parcelled out so no irrigation schemes work. The women do double
work in the fields, in their families, yet find time to paint.
Their walls picture Rama's wife Sita carried off by the demon
Ravanna in a palanquin, or today's bride, after puberty, being
carried to her husband's village, painted by Sita Devi, who was
married off at age twelve to a poor Brahmin priest, four daughters
dying in childhood, too undernourished (as girls often are) to fight
off the cholera. In despair, their mother turns to the powerful
Durga, and recites her a poem-prayer daily, and paints, the way
she once painted on her arms, her school slate, on the ground;
then was punished for wasting time. Now, during Bihar's 1968
famine from drought she's discovered. When she exhibits in Delhi
will Durga protect her so no one will cut off her hands out of jealousy?
Her son comes with her to D.C., eats ice cream with every meal,
even breakfast—just like my husband when he first came from India.
But I'd rather talk of philosophy, religion, abstract ideas, yet
reality intrudes. When I'm in India, I cover my plate with my
hands, rudely refusing what I might waste—because of the starving.

Gail Collins-Ranadive

Family stories entertained us before television, movies, radio, the Roxy, or Broadway shows.

We were scribes in Egypt, hence the name Siegel (Sigilium, the sealer). We were writers.

Mother's father rode the Russian plains on a white horse. Grandpa was the beloved, handsome, tall, improper skeptic. Grandma was the practical, yet romantic, reader of French novels, a believer in love and adventure but condemned to carry the weight of an orphaned family as a young widow with the door to adventure closed. But she was the grandma who found health spas and world fairs and far away markets and bargains and wholesale houses when her children were grown and had her own business.

Dad's father was a dapper Romanian, lover of women, sirer of half brothers and sisters from four or five alliances, who had one of the first cars in Philadelphia and a thriving business and my father, the entertainer, was the Marine hero who showed those southern boys on Okinawa that a New York City kid named Siegel could stand his ground and kill as well as any backwoods hunter.

Joan Starr

✣ FOURTEEN

I cut up this
harvest-moon/pumpkin
and plunge my hands
into all orange, the color
of strength and endurance,
slimy and cold

as the corpse that
my daughter dissects
in anatomy lab.
Now I place
a small candle
inside, try to
light it. It
flickers, goes out.
I try again,
singe my fingers
and smell my own flesh.
Heretic!
    Witch?
Fire gleams
through these eyes I've
created, turns the grin
into a leer.

Gail Collins-Ranadive

❧ FIFTEEN

She was a merchant. She was a very open, loving person with three children. She'd managed to make her two stores thrive and was well known in town.

One afternoon while she was at home alone, a knock came at the back door. Before she even had time to respond, he was through the door. A vagrant-type burst into the room and bludgeoned her to death, then punctured her body with knife stabs.

Cassie Arnold

94

Her husband was a trader. When the cavalry went out on an expedition, he followed at a safe distance, trading his goodies with the Indians behind the cavalry lines.

One time he was trading when the cavalry suddenly retreated, with hostile Indians in pursuit, and he was stuck there. Now he was outside the protection of the U.S. Army, and to survive he lived with the Indians and eventually became one of them.

He even married an Indian woman. It was expected of him, of course! Besides, who could tell whether he'd ever get back to that old hag at the Army post! By the time he returned, she was dead.

Rhea Kahn

He haunts himself, really, with his own twisted love of her, and his guilt. He opens the door between the worlds because, as the Navaho believe, a dark wind blows in his heart and she is only answering his call.

He can smell her sometimes and feel her in a room. When he concentrates she's gone. That's what is making him so crazy. He can't control it. It controls him. The dark wind holds them together.

Marsha Campbell

❧ SIXTEEN

Daily, I'm drawn
to this forest. Antlered
deer stare at me
through the trees, and I
think of Snow

White, the movie my real
mother took me to see.
I was sure we were going
instead to the dentist; after all,
it was Sunday, and movies
were sinful. Now in this
forest's silence of spider webs
dripping white mist, I recall
the awakening, feel
the apple dislodge from my throat,
sit up to look through
the glass dome. But I have
been silent so long, how
will I tell of this snake,
those frogs squawking into the water,
or these heron,
blue-grey in their hiding?

Gail Collins-Ranadive

SEVENTEEN

Traveling never has gotten me anywhere.
Always uprooted like a common onion
shedding old identities
 the certain security of the solid kitchen table
 the garden plot I nurtured with my own hands and dreams
 the familiar spring water, succulent and cool
 the friends to sustain me through each calamity.
Since the beginning, you see,

I've played his shadow
    rooted to him
        faceless
            with no name
merely Lot's wife
as much a part of his life
as Lot's coat or Lot's shoes.
There have even been times
when I've been boxed into silence
by his hardhanded decree:
"It will be better for us in _____
    Fill in the blank—
    any city or country will do.
Prosperity, for him,
is always over the next hill
and like lemmings
we follow this strange call.
As time has edged along, though,
we've become more distant.
Each move has been a cutting away
    discarding unused dreams
    turning our backs on withered entanglements.
Often I've lingered behind him
wanting to remember the laughter of a neighbor's child
    the buzz of the fruit market
    the chant of the spice dealer
and all the while I've longed
to claim and preserve
the daily harvests of my own life
    with more than mere memories
    or the heart-hardening salt of these tears.

Lenny Lianne

My sin has always been to devalue my own thoughts and feelings. As a child victim of incest, threatened with death if I told, I very quickly stockpiled my real thoughts and feelings. My mother, not consciously aware of what was happening, as far as I know, became my father's accomplice—an accomplice because she was not my ally.

How would I gain affirmation for my thinking and feeling if I'd only hold all inside, afraid for my own life?

Throughout my growing-up years I held thoughts and feelings close to me, protected them with my body, the pain locked in my cells. I could not outwardly be angry, although I could cry and not be abused for it. When I became a teenager, I did a lot of crying—crying ostensibly for my mother and my parents' dissolving relationship—crying for me as a victim of their disintegrating marriage.

Not until I was forty did I uncover the memories of incest—when a string of memories came to me in a workshop designed for individual and personal healing.

Since then, I have begun to discover just how much I devalued myself—and have begun to hold my feelings and thoughts in greater and greater esteem. Nevertheless, this remains the great sin of my life: there are places where I still hold out, hold on to this sin in subtle ways.

Debbie Taylor

NINETEEN

A butterfly symbolizes the cosmos for me. The metamorphosis of this insect in many ways parallels the constant changing, evolving force of the universe. In the pupae stage, so much of what is happening is hidden, unknown, just like the movements of continental plates, earthquakes, volcanoes. In the caterpillar stage we see something most people want to squash or birds eat them or they eat all the leaves off the trees. A very destructive or be destroyed stage—like storms, natural disasters, floods, heavy winds, avalanches. And then the butterfly emerges—a beautiful creature that gardeners try to attract into their yards with special plants. Frail creatures that soon soar to the heavens—like spirits. Ancient myths of many places thought butterflies were dead souls, waiting to be reborn. Butterflies are that spark in the cosmos that is the connecting tissue between souls.

Ada Churchill

TWENTY

The Moon is the face in my dark. My dark, which is deep
inside me, seeming (like the night sky) to have no end,
no door. The night sky is the vast nothingness of my soul,
and I am lost in it.
    My grief seems to have no end when
    I am lost in it, and seems to carry
    me nowhere.
Then, suddenly, there is a face in the dark,
and the moon of my knowing begins to traverse
the dark like a chariot, not of fire, but of ice.

Frozen water, illumination of a still quiet moment—
frozen for me to see and grasp it, like a still and silent
snapshot. The insight may be brief but I am able to
capture it with my pen, thank God.

Just as the moon, in a photo, holds a moment
of illumination still for me to remember:
to remember who I am: a soul with a face,
a face in my eternal dark.
Now I turn my face to the sun—source of my light.
For it is true that without the sun I would wither and die.
Oh sun, light my moon face, help me to see in this dark
nothingness. Give my moon the true knowledge that
I am alive, even in the darkest night.

Carolyn Cottom

All wound up around her, born under her sign, I get excited to see
her return. I call the others and we stand as she beams down that
magic connection.

Gradually, she slips away. Her fullness is enveloped by the
creeping darkness. Her bright face is shaded and she casts a dim-
mer light. The moon cycles around and comes back.

I think of many moons, bright or brooding, cloud-surrounded,
or moving across a clear deep and uncloud-fettered background.

Sometimes that small sliver of its last remnant seems to cut
through the cosmos, creating just enough opening through which
it does pour itself to fullness, on schedule, and start it all anew.

Cassie Arnold

100

TWENTY ONE

I often tell my children they are the best thing that ever happened to me. And they are. Being a mother has been so healing to me. I find I'm mothering myself in mothering them. That doesn't seem to make sense when you think of how much energy and patience they require, but I remember how taking a walk with a toddler slowed me down. Made me notice important things. Made me breathe easier and fuller. Made me feel whole and at peace. Both my children have the habit of coming to sit on my lap, upon awakening. And I sit there with this heavy, scented, warm bundle and can feel my heart beat as my child must and for me this holy prayer begins my day. No one and nothing else can be so consistently relied upon to get me to this place, this center.

Gloria Logan

TWENTY TWO

Get away from my desk
please
Go find your own space
please
No I won't be a kool-aid mom
clean the oven and the fridge
and give a shit about
twenty teenagers
think about dinner (and make it)
sit in the sun with
little girls just up from their naps
and listen to their dreams

and worry about my undone homework
while you do your paper
at my desk
why do I need to say *no*
in an explosion of
martyrdom
because I don't know how
to say yes to me yet in a
regular, sustained way
but I'm getting there.

Marsha Campbell

❧ TWENTY THREE

Exile—not from a country but from your
innermost core.
To wonder who you are apart from someone,
or will you disappear.
To fear being lost or are you already lost.
This is certainly the "Darkest Night of my Soul."
The pain at the bottom of that ever-moving
spiral—but is it the bottom? You only know
after you have begun to spiral up. Nothing
dramatic will happen—merely a change in view—
knowing you are coming home, home to yourself.

Vivian Barondes

TWENTY FOUR

Milo was his name. He valued me, needed me, treasured me,
read to me, fought for me—can you imagine, fought for me—
even took me to be his sacred daughter and legally adopted me.
I loved his mind, his very being. Naturally I would follow
in his path so I studied journalism. How natural it felt
that I, too, would one day become Chief-of-Staff of the
Associated Press, speak seven languages, play the violin—
become like him: as filled and fulfilled and giving.
He was magical and still is. His very being, even after
his death, is my force. How extraordinary that I knew him
only a year and a half.

Jeanne Gayler

He's strong, thin, lithe, dark, and bearded—he hides in his beard!
But what's inside comes out through his intensely burning dark
    eyes:
his wisdom, insightfulness, brilliance.
Is it wisdom, or is it rather his know-it-all attitude, which always
    scares me? It makes me back off, withdraw into safe, private,
    feminine ground.
Better be a good cook and mother, better scrub that dirty floor
    than allow that dark creature within to make his foray out
    into the sunlight, where he often gets me into trouble.

Rhea Kahn

TWENTY FIVE

It is a feeling that swells
within me as though from
the womb. Warm, moist, pulsating
with my own rebirth.
Needing no parental life seeds.
It gushes forth as a spring
from an unknown source.
It races over the rocks, glitters
in the sun and babbles with creation.

Miriam Phoebe Newton

I've been depressed over some winters,
but during the last couple I've settled
into the quietness, somber tones, early
darkness and found peace and beauty here.
　　Now when I see the first crocus
peeping its head out I resist. I'm not
ready for spring. I resent all these brightly
blooming daffodils.
　　Spring's born for me like a baby—
once begun it comes on fast and furious
and there's no stopping now and hardly
time to catch a breath.

Gloria Logan

Spring dances across the stage claiming, "My turn." "My time." "I've waited in the wings, I've prepared my inner core, I've held my mystery and now it's my moment!" "Watch me perform." "Watch my wonder, look at my color." "I'll thrill you. Just stand and watch!"

Jeanne Gayler

❧ TWENTY SIX

At some point every spring there is an instant when there is a smell in the air at a certain place—a smell not like anything else I know. I can't name it, maybe because it is the combination of everything at that particular place and that moment. Or maybe it is the earth calling with its symphony of the senses. And it is then that it is time to get out in my garden. Time to put on my oldest clothes and oldest shoes and time to put my hair back. It is time to put my hands in the dirt. My mother the earth is calling. I am renewed.

Vivian Barondes

My heaven is a place of tranquility; a place where I can refresh my mind, rejuvenate my body, and renew my spirit so that the day-to-day absurdities of life become bearable and even accepted as part of living. My home is a holy place because I can touch heaven there. I love to see the bright sun streaming through the windows; I love to hear the cool, clean water flowing in our aquarium; I love to watch the birds and the squirrels just outside my kitchen window feasting on sunflower seeds; I love my gardens, where I have tilled and toiled for the past twelve years.

But something has happened to my holy place. It's been invaded by little men. Little men who think of me as Mama. They follow me around, expect me to play with them, fix their meals, do their laundry, clean their noses, dry their tears, hold them, protect them. All of which I do....

It is no longer easy to hold a quiet conversation with my husband. It is no longer easy to even finish a thought. And for a while, it was not easy to touch Heaven around my home. There is evidence in every room and even in my gardens of little men invasions. But I've come to realize that my two little boys are part of my heaven now. I share it with them—and with their trucks in the garden, their balls in the goldfish pond, their socks under the table.

Brenda Tuttle

❧ TWENTY SEVEN

The reason I'm such a goddamn pleaser is because
it is hell for me to be in a place with people
where they are displeased with me or mad at me.
I can't stand being a disappointer. It is hell
for me to be abandoned emotionally by people I
love. I know this grows directly out of my
experience of my mother's death. But I'm learning
to live in hell and face my damnation directly.
Because the price I pay by having to be everything
for everybody else is too dear. Yet it is such
a struggle for me. And always will be.

Gloria Logan

106

In my private Hell, everyone has turned their backs on me—or worse, they sit stone-faced in a circle, then turn and whisper "sweet everythings" in each other's ears.

In daily moments, Hell wears the face of my teenage children, when they ignore me or answer my earnest questions with bitter sarcasm—as if to say, "Who are you to want to be a part of my life?"

It wears the face of my lover—or rather, his absence, the lack of his face—when I am needing and wanting affirmation that I am not alone.

In my private Hell, death is Nothing, does not frighten me wearing its bony white mask. It is rather the sense that no one is there for me. Everyone is in love with everyone else, and I alone am isolated, separated by a thick black veil.

Carolyn Cottom

❧ TWENTY EIGHT

What if we were really tolerant of differences—different religions, values, languages, and cultural practices?

What if we stood together and said *no* to those who would take away the rights of others?

What if all children were viewed as our own children, so that no child was allowed to be hungry or homeless, uneducated or without health care?

What if we insisted that time and space be made for family life; time for caring for our elderly; for spending time together; time for meeting child and healthcare needs without financial devastation?

What would happen if we placed greater value on people's actions than on their possessions or positions of power?

What if to live simply was applauded?
What if we valued accomplishment in the home or personal
    relationships as much as we value accomplishments in the
    world of work?
What if we supported artists so their visions could be shared
    more widely?
What if we encouraged creativity in everyone?

Eloise Singh

We're making progress in our family.
Women are already in the temple.
They are writing hymnals,
Singing the sacred songs,
and sitting at the head table with the VIPs.
Our gatekeeper opens the door for everyone to come in.
We've an easy access ramp for the handicapped,
Child-sized furniture for the children,
There are roles for everyone in the passion play.
Some men are afraid and stand outside in the rain.
Sullen and afraid to *come in*
They *peek in* at the windows
Mock the services as trivial
The architecture as derivative.
They are hungry and we wish to share bread.
They are thirsty and we have holy water.
Come and take communion with us, in peace.
Let this earth be a house for *all*.
Welcome home.

Joan Starr

Prior to my job interview I went to the Louisville equivalent of Woodies and paid a modest $250 for an interview suit. I paid another $50 for a pair of black Joyce pumps. My hair was cut at one of the most prestigious hairstylists. I interviewed for the job as a staff attorney and was hired.

Now I have torn the shoulder pads out of the jacket. I do not wear the black herringbone A-line skirt, and the black Joyce pumps sit in the closet, gathering dust. The women who ride the elevator in my office building all wear varying degrees of the professional garb. I particularly notice the shoes—a different pump for every pompadour.

The pump—that vicious little animal that bites women's toes and keeps them off balance all day—ankles swollen and hurting in the evening. Men should have to wear them for a year. The pump is for western wear the equivalent of the Chinese binding of feet. What if we all let our feet spread out to their full stature? My friend wears size 9-D sandals—would that my feet will grow to that size!

Rose Ashcraft

I am increasingly uncomfortable in suits. I don my suit of armor and become a gladiator, too often orating a position that I do not agree with. I think of yesterday of my cross-examination of a woman with bipolar disorder. Does the national security require that she lose her security clearance and her job? Am I complicit? I don my suit. I stand behind the podium. I play this role for five hours without even being allowed a break for lunch. After it's over, a friend who observed does not congratulate me on my performance; she feels sorry for the woman who looked defensive under my cross-examination. I go home and take off the suit.

Kathy Braeman

❧ THIRTY

It was early fall and I was with friends, horsing around in the water at the foot of a large waterfall. This state park was a popular spot and I'd often stepped into the water here, but today was the first time I actually swam in it. I climbed out of the water, scooted up an embankment, and then jumped down into the water from a height of, say, six feet. I did it again and again. I swam right under the waterfall, where I listened to its roar and found the spot in the middle where no water fell. The afternoon sun was going down and I should have been chilled but instead I was warm with excitement, with this new brave self.

Karen Bennett

❧ THIRTY ONE

Here are some things I have learned.

> It is autumn now, and winter will follow.
> By the end of this workday, I will be tired.
> If I eat less, I will lose weight.
> When my boss leaves to take a new job, I will find it stressful to adjust to a new boss.

Somehow as I grew up, I missed important truths that are implicit in the statements above. I did not know that the present will change: I will grow older, spring will follow winter. And I did not understand the idea of free choice. Instead, I experienced the choices I made as compulsions, actions about which I had no choice. However, I didn't know that I didn't know these things. Only recently have I discovered time, and my own important place in my life story.

Susan Holst

❧ THIRTY TWO

I resent change, so I am a terrible student. When someone tries to show me something new, inside I am thinking, "How dare you tell me what to do! I know what to do! I am smart! I am experienced! I can't stand the idea that you have something I don't have." Because of this Herod part of me, I have had to teach myself almost everything I know. I know much less than I would if I could learn from those around me.

Susan Holst

❧ THIRTY THREE

When the angel craze grew up in the late eighties, Ann asked if I believed. Rational humanist that I was at that time, I thought about it: About how this woman who had flown with the WASPs during World War II had become my writing teacher, then mentor, and now was providing me someplace to live while I began my writing/teaching career, then replied, "Yes, you are an angel in my life." She dismissed this as nonsense, but I've been counting angels ever since.

Gail Collins-Ranadive

THIRTY FOUR

The view is just for me. Out my window the road cuts through the yellow trees, and the church steeple points its white arrow into the big blue sky. On the train, no one watches me as I scan their faces: they are deep in newspapers and books, listening to their earphones, staring into middle spaces, fixing their clothes, eating. Their faces, all different, hang sweetly before me, live portraits in a museum.

Susan Holst

THIRTY FIVE

I appreciate the fact that I can rise out of my chair, lift one foot and put it down in front of the other until I have walked out of this room, out of my house, and into the street. In the street, it is calm now: There are no explosions, no fire or flood. I can walk to the grocery store, where I find fresh oranges and other fruits arranged in fragile pyramids. In my wallet is money to buy the fruit and other foods I enjoy. When I return home, I will eat my food and drink a glass of water, swallowing each gulp and feeling the cool liquid move through my esophagus and into my stomach.

Karen Bennett

112

THIRTY SIX

For Olympia Brown
(the first American woman denominationally ordained
into the ministry, by the Universalists, in 1863)

Today I begin your biography
early. It's snowing, though
spring. I relive this season
in Europe, awaiting acceptance
by your Antioch. In the
snow rain sleet hail
of that spring there was only
one truth: your trinity of womanhood
fool, angel, drudge
going to army wives' teas.
This week's rain drips from tree
branches, flows over lawns, down
gutters, gurgles under the streets,
tributary streams of your second trinity:
experience instruction inspiration
for you becoming one in the ministry.
I struggle through seasons of fear
that the "unseen" within be forever forsaken.
New blossoms bloat on the tree limbs
and still it is snowing. This is
the feminine season: moisture puddles
in this field of time. Sleet starts again
and the sacred heads wounded are
those of the earliest daffodils.

Gail Collins-Ranadive

Harriet Tubman

I feel like I could write her story, because I have felt like a spy and an underground guerrilla in this man's world. I am, like her, a survivor of a kind of slavery. And we walked at night feeling our way through the darkness—led by moss growing on the north side of trees and the light of our faith in that which is Divine. Moss and trees, darkness and hope and the courage of a few who dared to help.

Marsha Campbell

🦋 THIRTY SEVEN

In the beginning there was darkness, and chaos, and Mind. Mind wandered about in the darkness, bumping into Chaos, stumbling over and around Chaos until there was nothing left to do but put Chaos in order. In the process of organizing Chaos, Mind would once in a while catch a glimpse of a small brightness in the Dark. Gradually, little by little, the brightness became focused into a spark. The spark became clearer, and brighter and became Spirit, who joined Mind in organizing Chaos.

Spirit and Mind wandered on through the Dark until they felt themselves more joined together in their search. They built themselves a protective coating—a body—they put on arms and legs—they became Person—Mind/Spirit/Body.

Person multiplied and became fruitful and Spirit became Universal Consciousness. Mind became all the Sciences and Organizations. All are still careful to guard unconditional Love which is the basic force of all Life.

Ada Churchill

114

I am the face of the deep that darkness falls upon.
I split and from my being springs the light but it
is not such a big deal. For I spring up light in
sweet and sprightly ways. I don't exude. I bubble.
I giggle forth happy children of light. And they dance
and they eat and they tire and nestle closely together
and I feel their breath on my endless neck. They dig
into me with their hands and form little pockets of light
in my darkness. They hide in me and I push them back out
into the light. Sometimes they cry because it is too bright.
I receive them always.

                                        Beth Hudson Latture

THIRTY EIGHT

It was always here when it seemed most absent. My seeing doesn't make it real. The pale yellow possibility of translucent autumn leaves sleeps inside summer green and bare winter wood. Perhaps I am the thing that changes. The seasons of my grief, joy, peace, and tempest are not regular but always I am myself. And through it all there is an eternity that knows unalterably who I am. And like the universe, I am cyclical. Together the world and I circle the source of life, sometimes cold and dark, sometimes bright and warm, we are all held in ceaseless orbit, returning endlessly to ourselves and the axis of the unchanging.

                                        Maria Bates

THIRTY NINE

Being rocked in a mother's arms.
Being loved beyond anything.
Feeling peace at being connected.
The sacred is the quiet place.
The deepest place. The most loving place.

Gloria Logan

One is the name with the power
to make sacred special places
when full of holy energy the hands
transmute the dross into gold,
the light into dark
the dark into rainbow
the nightmare into paradise
One plays with the colors, smell and taste
bringing all into orbit
dancing from ring to ring.

Joan Starr

❧ FORTY

First thing each morning, I will take my cup of hot coffee into the living room where I will listen to Bach for fifteen minutes as I write in my journal.

Karen Bennett

Awakening to an early spring
snow fearing winter can regain
its hold, the budding forsythia
again become sticks on which
to hang eggs red from other
crushed springs, shared instinct
says *no*! The cultivated forsythia's
been with us so long it mirrors
our human behavior: Inner sparks,
once started, become little
bursts of the sun, shaped like
the stars we all come from. Though
some have been burned by the cold,
bruised by snow, spring's message
is not of a martyred dying
but of the will to survive, bearing
witness to life; and with the forsythia,
we find ourselves flowering with hope.

Gail Collins-Ranadive

RESOURCES

Barth, Edna. *Lilies, Rabbits, and Painted Eggs: The Story of the Easter Symbols.* New York: Clarion Books, 2001.

Bennett, Anne McGrew. *From Woman-Pain to Woman-Vision.* Ed. Mary E. Hunt. Minneapolis: Fortress Press, 1989.

Bolen, Jean Shinoda. *Crossing to Avalon: A Woman's Midlife Pilgrimmage.* San Francisco: HarperSan Francisco, 1995.

Bolen, Jean Shinoda. *Goddesses in Everywoman.* New York: Harper and Row, 1984.

Bolen, Jean Shinoda. *The Tao of Psychology: Synchronicity and the Self.* San Francisco: HarperSan Francisco, 1982.

Boulding, Elise. *The Underside of History: A View of Women Through Time.* Boulder: Westview Press, 1976.

Campbell, Joseph. *The Inner Reaches of Outer Space: Metaphor as Myth and as Religion.* Novato, CA: New World Library, 2002.

Campbell, Joseph. *Myths To Live By.* London: Arkana, 1993.

Christ, Carol. *Diving Deep and Surfacing: Women Writers on Spiritual Quest.* Boston: Beacon Press, 1995.

Christ, Carol and Judith Plaskow, Ed. *Womanspirit Rising.* San Francisco: HarperSan Francisco, 1992.

Cooney, Robert and Helen Michalowski, Ed. *The Power of the People: Active Nonviolence in the United States.* Philadelphia: New Society Publishers, 1987.

de Castillejo, Irene Claremont. *Knowing Woman.* Boston: Shambhala Publications, 1997.

Donnelly, Dody H. *Radical Love: An Approach to Sexual Spirituality.* Fremont, CA: Dharma Cloud Publishers, 1993.

Edinger, Edward F. *Ego and the Archetype: Individuation and the Religious Function of the Psych.* Boston: Shambhala Publications, 1992.

Friedman, Edwin H. *Generation to Generation.* New York: Guilford Press, 1985.

Gilligan, Carol. *In a Different Voice*. Cambridge, MA: Harvard University Press, 1993.

Harding, M. Ester. *Woman's Mysteries*. New York: Bantam, 1973.

Hirshfield, Jane, Ed. *Women in Praise of the Sacred: 43 Centuries of Spiritual Poetry by Women*. New York: HarperCollins, 1994.

Hopkins, Patricia and Sherry Ruth Anderson. *The Feminine Face of God: The Unfolding of the Sacred in Women*. New York: Bantam Doubleday Dell, 1992.

Leshan, Lawrence. *How to Meditate: A Guide to Self-Discovery*. Boston: Little, Brown & Co., 1999.

Moessner, Jeanne Stevenson, Ed. *Through the Eyes of Women: Insights for Pastoral Care*. Minneapolis: Fortress Press, 1996.

Morton, Nelle. *The Journey Is Home*. Boston: Beacon Press, 1986.

Mumford, Lewis. *The Myth of the Machine*. New York: Harcourt, Brace and World, Inc., 1962.

Ostriker, Alicia Suskin. *Stealing the Language*. Boston: Beacon Press, 1987.

Pratt, Annis. *Archetypal Patterns in Women's Fiction*. Bloomington: Indiana University Press, 1981.

Roberts, Bernadette. *The Path to No-Self: Life at the Center*. Albany, NY: State University of New York Press, 1992.

Sanford, John A. *The Invisible Partners*. New York: Paulist Press, 1984.

Sarton, May. *Writings on Writing*. Orono, ME: Puckerbrush Press, 1980.

Taylor, Jeremy. *Dream Work: Techniques for Discovering the Creative Power in Dreams*. New York: Paulist Press, 1984.

Walker, Barbara G. *The Woman's Dictionary of Symbols and Sacred Objects*. San Francisco: HarperSan Francisco, 1988.

Walker, Barbara G. *The Woman's Encyclopedia of Myths and Secrets*. San Francisco: HarperSan Francisco, 1983.

Woolf, Virginia. *A Room of One's Own*. New York: Harcourt Brace, 1991.

Woolf, Virginia. *Three Guineas*. New York: Harcourt Brace Jovanovich, Inc., 1966.